BOYE

Each year the ABC invites a prominent Australian to present the result of his or her work and thinking on major social, scientific or cultural issues in a series of radio talks known as the Boyer Lectures. The series was inaugurated in 1959 under the title of the ABC Lectures but in 1961 was renamed as a memorial to the late Sir Richard Boyer, who as chairman of the ABC had been one of those responsible for its introduction.

VOICES FROM THE LAND

The 1993 Boyer Lectures offer some visions of the future for Aboriginal and Islander life in Australia. The seven Aboriginal and Torres Strait Islander lecturers talk about medicine, law, education, the media, politics and linguistics.

VOICES FROM THE LAND

Mandawuy Yunupingu • Dot West
Ian Anderson • Jeanie Bell
Getano Lui (Jnr) • Helen Corbett
Noel Pearson

an ABC BOOK

Published by ABC Books for the
AUSTRALIAN BROADCASTING CORPORATION
GPO Box 9994 Sydney NSW 2001

First published 1994

National Library of Australia
Cataloguing-in-Publication entry
Voices from the land.

ISBN 0 7333 0344 7.

[1.] Aborigines, Australian – Social conditions. 2. Torres Strait Islanders – Social conditions. 3. Australia – Social conditions – 1990– . I. Yunupingu, Mandawuy. II. Australian Broadcasting Corporation. (Series: Boyer lectures; 1993).

305.89915

Designed by Helen Semmler
Set in 11/13pt Berkeley Old Style
by Midland Typesetters, Maryborough, Victoria
Printed and bound in Australia by
Australian Print Group, Maryborough, Victoria

2-1695

10 9 8 7 6 5 4 3 2 1

Voices From the Land was produced for ABC Radio National by Linden Woodward and Ursula Raymond

CONTENTS

THE LECTURERS

MANDAWUY YUNUPINGU is best known as the lead singer/songwriter of Yothu Yindi, Australia's most successful Aboriginal band. He is also a traditional owner of Gumatj land in Arnhem Land, and is principal of Yirrkala school.

Mr Yunupingu was a member of the 1988 National Aboriginal Education Taskforce charged with the responsibility of writing the national Aboriginal education policy. He has also been involved in education issues in the Northern Territory, and with Batchelor College—an Aboriginal College of TAFE which offers degree courses in education.

DOT WEST is Chairperson of the National Indigenous Media Association of Australia, and Training and Broadcasting Coordinator for the Broome Aboriginal Media Association. She presents a weekly program on Radio Goolarri in Broome—one of more than one hundred Aboriginal radio programs in Australia. Ms West started in broadcasting as a volunteer in 1988, and later took up a traineeship at Waringarri Media in Kununurra. She has gone on to work for indigenous media at a national level, campaigning for the expansion and consolidation of the Aboriginal media network.

DR IAN ANDERSON is one of fewer than ten Aboriginal medical graduates in Australia. He graduated from the University of Melbourne in 1989, and is the author of *Koorie Health in Koorie Hands*. Dr Anderson works at the Victorian Aboriginal Health Service and does some teaching on Aboriginal health at the University of Melbourne. He is pursuing post-graduate studies in sociology and anthropology at La Trobe University.

JEANIE BELL graduated as a linguist from Monash University in 1980, and is one of the few Aboriginal linguists in Australia. She worked as Coordinator of the Centre for Aboriginal and Islander Studies at the University of Queensland, and has worked in the language section of the Institute for Aboriginal Development in Alice Springs.

Ms Bell is a member of the Federation of Aboriginal and Torres Strait Islander Languages, as well as the Australian Languages and Literacy Council. She is currently researching dictionaries of Butchulla (Fraser Islander) and Gubbi Gubbi (Mary River, S E Qld) languages.

GETANO LUI (JNR) is a very active community leader in the Torres Strait. He is chairman of the Island Coordinating Council, the Torres Strait Regional Council, and the Island Board of Industry and Service. He is also a member of a number of other regional, national and international groups. Mr Lui has spoken widely on the cultural and political life of the Torres Strait.

HELEN CORBETT was co-founder of the National Committee to Defend Black Rights, and has been a key campaigner on the issue of Aboriginal deaths in custody. She is Vice-President of the Unrepresented Nations and Peoples Organisation, and has a long career in local, state, national and international campaigns on Aboriginal issues.

She has worked for Aboriginal medical, legal, educational and children's services, and has also been involved in the peace and nuclear disarmament movement. She is a representative on the World Council of Indigenous Peoples, and is the Aboriginal delegate to the Council's Women's Commission. She has been involved with the United Nations Working Group on Indigenous Populations since 1987.

NOEL PEARSON is from the Hopevale community on Cape York Peninsula. He has an honours degree in history from Sydney University, and completed a law degree in 1993. Mr Pearson was an advisor to the Hopevale Aboriginal Council, and helped establish the Cape York Land Council in 1990. He was part of the Queensland Government's working group to establish the 1991 Aborignal Land Act, but resigned in protest over deficiencies in the proposed legislation. Noel Pearson is Executive Director of the Cape York Land Council, based in Cairns. His essay '204 Years of Invisible Title' is included in the recent publication *Mabo: A Judicial Revolution.* He was one of the team who dealt with the Federal Government on its response to the Mabo Native Title decision.

One

YOTHU YINDI—FINDING BALANCE

Mandawuy Yunupingu

I want to talk about education but first I want to talk about Yothu Yindi. We are a band with a philosophy. Yothu Yindi is the name of a fundamental concept in our Yolngu life. For us Aboriginal people of Arnhemland the name Yothu Yindi conjures up the idea of balance, a harmony we actively work at.

We took the name Yothu Yindi for the band because it is the name of an important relationship in our kinship system. In this kinship system the land and its peoples are divided into two sides—the Yirritja and the Dhuwa. Our life is dedicated to maintaining balance between these. For us, when Yirritja and Dhuwa are working in harmony the land and its peoples are one.

Our kinship system links Aboriginal Australians across most of the Top End of the Northern Territory. It also links in many white Australians who have been willingly adopted. These myriad families make up a mesh of inter-relations between people and land. We take the balance of nature as our inspiration.

Yothu Yindi refers to the child and its mother. But to understand the full importance of Yothu Yindi you need to know a bit more. Dhuwa mothers have Yirritja children and

Yirritja mothers have Dhuwa children. Or to see it from the child's point of view, every Dhuwa child has Yirritja mothers and Dhuwa fathers, and every Yirritja child has Dhuwa mothers and Yirritja fathers. Every Yolngu child has responsibilities both to mother's people and places and to father's people and places. Hence every Yolngu person has responsibilities both to Yirritja and to Dhuwa.

In our band Yothu Yindi we have a balance between Yirritja and Dhuwa. But we also have another balance, one between black and white, or Yolngu and Balanda. Amongst the Yirritja members of our band there are both black and white, and among the Dhuwa members of our band there are both black and white.

Keep the notion of balance in mind. A dynamic balance such as we see in nature.

With balance in mind I want to tell you a story about education, my own education and the education that my children are having. Telling you this story tells you how Yothu Yindi the band came about and how it became a contemporary voice for us Yolngu.

My own education was a Yolngu education. It took place with our large family group living in the places on our land that hold special importance for us. With Mum and Dad we went from place to place, and every place had its stories. Some of these were sacred stories that we heard sung in ceremonies. Some were family stories, like Mum's stories of when she was a little girl in this place or that. We knew that my grandad had been here, and his grandad before him did these things, and right back to the ancestors who made the land as they went about doing just the same sorts of things we did in our ordinary life and in our ceremonial life.

Mum and Dad travelled long distances with us kids. Just by going and living in the various places we were respecting those ancestors of ours who made the world. My father followed the seasons in his lands. Sometimes Mum took us over to her places. Like during April when it was starting to get chilly at night we would be inland. We were in covered places where it was sheltered; all those cosy places. We would camp there in the jungle and get honey from beehives in the rocks—rock honey. When the cold snap was coming on, after April into May/June when it is almost going into the dry season, that's when we'd start hanging around there.

Even when we were camped inland we would come down to the beach. There were good spots there. We would get Mum to come and help us collect oysters and get honey—rock honey—and fruit, traditional fruit in season. Just like now, when we go to places to collect fruits, say at Galaru just north of where Nhulunbuy township is, it's a form of homage and recognition for the Djankawu sisters, those ancestral women who did the same thing there in their world-making activity.

Each move was a change of context as far as my education was concerned. Each new place has new concepts associated with it. Each place is connected to other places in deep ways. And I learned about that, both from being in the place and by associating it with the songs and dances of our ceremonies. In this way, the more abstract knowledge of how places are connected was linked with the practical and emotional knowledge of actually living in a place.

My father would teach me to be a man and take me hunting, spear fishing. He taught me all the fish names. And he would tell me off for doing naughty things too.

I remember the night-times best. We would listen to stories at night by the campfire. All the stories had a strong lesson for us kids. They would be stories to get us to stay put by the fire and not wander about. They would get us frightened and get us to sleep much faster.

This is the 'fifties and early 'sixties I'm remembering. But, as I grew, our Yolngu world was no longer ours alone. Changes in my family's lifestyle were taking place. Influences outside the family and clan were being felt. Both Yirritja and Dhuwa people were being moved around by white people. Clans were being assembled here and encouraged to leave there. The missionaries had been around all my life. Somehow they started to have more impact on us all.

About this time my fathers and uncles and my older brother were involved with the court challenge to the Government of Australia and NABALCO, the big foreign mining company that wanted our land. The struggle was to find ways of explaining our laws and beliefs to white Australia in an attempt to retain all that is important and sacred in Yolngu life—our land. That struggle to explain our laws and beliefs is what you hear in Yothu Yindi's songs today. In our songs we have found a way to help people hear us today. But back then it wasn't possible.

After my initiation I began to go to school regularly. It was all quite funny to me at the time. But it had its exciting bits. As I see it now I needed this different sort of energy, different learning. But a whole lot went along with it, like having to wear clothes. Sometimes when I had no shorts I'd wear *naga*. It didn't worry me. The missionaries had their 'young ladies', the Yolngu girls' sewing class, make our uniforms for us.

Sometimes I found aspects of education really good; I learned something new. It was like every day you were looking at things, and then you were challenged. I'd try to match it. I could practically hear my brain working. But sometimes I found the classroom isolated, cut off from everything I knew and loved. I'd sit in that school for five or twenty minutes and then go back home and play to our own rules.

School worked for me. For my type of thinking Western education could fit in. I think my parents had it fixed in their minds, too, that I should be schooled in order to give me a good balanced education.

Learning English just kept me coming back for more. I remember learning lots of bible words. Learning English was a pleasure. I already knew ten or so clan languages and English was a great new challenge. I remember coming back to the family with new English words which I'd try out on them. I distinctly remember showing-off to my sisters by reciting 'The House that Jack Built'.

But looking back now I can see that the teachers probably saw things differently to me. Many of their demands were quite incomprehensible. They weren't just teaching me 'useful things'; they had a theory, an ideology. I see now that it was a curriculum driven by the ideology of assimilation. I marvel at the ways we knew how to resist it. I see now that a lot of what motivated those white teachers was the view that it was only when Yolngu stop being Yolngu that we could become Australians.

But what about schooling now? Have schools stopped being the instrument of assimilation? My children are in school. I became the principal of the school where I once sat at a desk with the other Yolngu kids. Are my kids having a Yolngu education comparable in depth and rigour to what my parents gave me? I would answer a firm yes. But I can only answer yes because for nearly a quarter of a century people, both Yolngu and Balanda, have worked to achieve this. We have transformed the missionary, assimilation ideology into an authentic Yolngu schooling. It took a lot of imagination and struggle.

The changes which we have introduced into our schools did not just happen. Since the early 1970s a large group of people have made it happen. They have had a different vision and have struggled with those whose imaginations are more limited. Yolngu and Balanda who are now old men and women have been involved.

I'm thinking of people like our old Balanda friend Nugget Coombs, who recently spoke at a Melbourne University graduation ceremony at Yirrkala. He recalled his involvement with our community over the past twenty-five years. I'm thinking of people like my relation, Dambalipu, who told Education Department officials we needed schools in the new homelands settlements we were establishing in the 1970s. They just couldn't understand why we wanted to leave the big mission settlements for our traditional homelands. But still we started schools in those homelands with our own people as teachers. The Department officials were puzzled and amazed.

Each of our clans has its own homelands. And in the 1970s we began to establish different life ways in our own homelands, blending old ways and new. Naturally we want our children to be reared at home. But should a child have to miss out on schooling just because the family wants him or her to grow up at home?

In the bureaucratic minds of Department officials schools were associated with being away from all things Aboriginal. Schools in homelands centres upset all their categories. And I know from painful experience that when you upset white people's categories you'd better watch out.

In our struggle we have always had Yolngu concepts to guide us. I'm going to tell you about one of them—the concept of *Ngathu*. *Ngathu* is the name of the sacred bread we bake from the flour of the nuts of the cycad palm.

Some years ago we were searching for ways of coming up with a Yolngu curriculum for our schools. We needed something to expand our imaginations. Something which would lead us to do things in proper ways. We wanted to create a Yolngu curriculum which our community would feel was theirs. Two elders who were working with us, my older sister Gulumbu and her husband Djamika, told us to remember the process of *ngathu*. It could help us find the ways to do things which would produce a sustaining 'bread' for children, matched to their differing needs as learners.

The making of *ngathu* begins in particular cycad groves. Only particular groups of people may harvest the nuts and prepare the bread. Others are represented in the process through their relations with those actually doing the work. *Ngathu* is sacred because it contains something of the spirit of the ancestors left in the place where the cycad trees grow. People's work and our established ways of doing things and respect and judgement are also baked into the *ngathu*.

After collecting the big yellow and red nuts they are carried to a place for processing; not just any place. And the nuts are shelled. The kernels are sorted into three or four piles depending on size and colour. These will each make bread of a different type. Mixed with wood ash from a particular type of tree, the flesh is baked in the sun for two days.

The next stage must also occur in a particular place. In their special woven bags the kernels must be immersed in a pool with clear running water for some days. This process washes away the poison—cyanide—which is in the flesh. How long are they left? This depends on the nuts, the ash, the flow of water through the pool, the weather. It's a particular degree of hardness in the flesh that the women are testing for when they check. Of course, the older and more experienced women are those whose opinions are most respected in this matter.

The nuts are ground with two stones. Each category of nuts must be ground separately. Different groups of people will receive each type of bread depending on their particular relations with the cycad grove from which the collections were made. The dough is wrapped in thick sheets of paper bark and secured with bark string. The packages are placed in the hot ashes. The cooked bread will keep for many weeks. When I was young there were ceremonies with many, many people from all around who were fed throughout the ceremony on this bread.

I am telling you this because I think the *ngathu* analogy can serve as an inspiration for the work ahead of all of us as Australians. Work we need to do as we begin to think and talk about reconciliation between black and white Australians, and becoming a republic.

How is a curriculum, or for that matter an agreement over reconciliation, or the constitution of a new republic, like a loaf of *ngathu* bread?

Often we Yolngu talk of natural processes or of the ordinary everyday practices as fundamental to Yolngu life.

But you should not think that this means that it is only practical things that matter in Aboriginal life. We are talking about natural processes but meaning at another level.

We gather all the nuts from a particular place. We seek the focussed but varied opinions and views of people about schooling. Ideas must be put into relation with each other and sorted. The sub-categories and different sorts of issues should be separated so that things can go on in an orderly way. And then when the mix is ready it must be left for a while. How long? The time will depend on the conditions. Who will know when it is ready to act on? When will the flesh be ready for grinding? When all the bad blood of disagreement has leached away. We must accept the verdict of those we trust as experienced and who are in the right position and place to decide.

The sacred cycad nuts are represented in the form of the *ngathu*. It is presented in ritual ways to those whose various interests are embedded in the bread. Remembering the preparation of *ngathu* reminds us that there are right and wrong ways. Hurry, and the poison will remain in the bread. There are ways of proceeding that, structurally, ensure that the interests of all are recognised and respected.

Now another story which has helped us and inspired us is *Ganma*. When I think of *Ganma* I see the 'tri symbol'. I guess you could call it a triangle but it's not the angles which are important, it's the points and how they express for Yolngu the idea of knowledge. It's the linkages, and how they are made, that are important.

Also, talk of *Ganma* brings another image to my mind. A deep pool of brackish water, fresh water and salt water mixed. The pool is a balance between two different natural patterns, the pattern of the tidal flow, salt water moving in through the mangrove channels, and the pattern of the fresh water streams varying in their flow across the wet and dry seasons. Often when I describe this vision to Balanda, non-Aboriginal people, they wrinkle up their noses. For Balanda, brackish water is distasteful. But for us the sight and smell of brackish water expresses a profound foundation of useful knowledge—balance. For Yolngu Aboriginal people brackish water is a source of inspiration.

In each of the sources of flowing water there is ebb and flow. The deep pool of brackish water is a complex dynamic balance. In the same ways, balance of Yolngu life is achieved through ebb and flow of competing interests, through our elaborate kinship system. And I feel that in the same ways balance between black and white in Australia can be achieved.

Ganma is a metaphor. We are talking about natural processes but meaning at another level. *Ganma* is social theory. It is our traditional profound and detailed model of how what Europeans call 'society' works.

Of course Europeans have society and nature as quite different and opposed things. But for us, society and nature are *not* separate. We have Yirritja and Dhuwa, and these categories contain elements which are both natural and social. Also, of course, they have elements which Europeans call supernatural or metaphysical.

Now this is the place for me to sum things up.

Like many people of my age all over the world I see that my children's lives are different to my life as a child. My children are in Yolngu schools taught by Yolngu teachers.

Like me, my wife Yalmay is a teacher. We are both trained in the Balanda sense, but we are also guided by Yolngu elders. We are gradually making our schools into Yolngu institutions.

It seems to us that the most important thing is language. Our children study their clan languages in school. They learn to understand the deep meanings and to read and write in their mother's and father's languages. We also think that the study of English language is important for our children. It holds a significant place in our curriculum. But it is placed within a curriculum of multiple balances. Balances that our children must learn if they are going to be active Aboriginal members of our contemporary Australia.

Mathematics is important too. In fact we have spent a lot

of time and words developing a maths curriculum for our kids, a genuine Aboriginal mathematics. We have called this a Ganma Maths Curriculum and it is in the process of being officially recognised as an approved course of study in mathematics. It enables our children to work intellectually with the balances they must achieve in their lives.

Yolngu education is a balanced, active process. We have come a long way since I was a child. And Yothu Yindi, the band, came directly out of that struggle to find our Yolngu voice in the contemporary world.

Balance between different points of view is possible. That's what our Yolngu life is all about. Balancing difference between Yirritja and Dhuwa, between women and men and so on. Aboriginal and non-Aboriginal Australians can value and protect their differences while still finding ways to work at balance.

Governments and institutions need to see and to find ways of working with different knowledges. Part of this is beginning to see European-type knowledge as just one sort of knowledge among many. The land rights legislation and now the High Court ruling in the Mabo case have begun this.

Some white Australians are beginning to accept that European and Aboriginal ways of knowing have different logics. Non-Aboriginal people need to take time and make the effort to understand the logic of Aboriginal knowledge.

Active participation of Aboriginal peoples will renew Australian life during the twenty-first century. But it will need Aboriginal people who are strong and balanced, rooted in their families and their land. This will depend on Aboriginal people being educated as balanced contemporary Aboriginal Australians, something which will only happen when this education is inspired by their land.

In concluding, I remind you that we're living in fluid times, trying to discover in more profound ways what it is to be Australian. I think the vast majority of Australians would agree that Aboriginal Australians have a special contribution to make to that. But there seems to be a problem. I think most non-Aboriginal Australians accept that there is a deep intellectual strength to Aboriginal knowledge, but they seem to think of it as a mystery. I hope we are less of a mystery now. I have tried to help you see something of the ways that the concepts through which Aboriginal life is guided come from the processes of the land.

Your parents and grandparents saw us as utterly mysterious and incomprehensible. For you lot we had to be different and inferior, otherwise your lot could not have treated us the way they did. They refused to see us as civilised people who owned land. Your lot wanted us to be just a blur on the land, like a smudge on paper that could be rubbed out. That was an important part of your colonising us.

I am saying that it is time for those attitudes to be left behind. It is time you understood us as we are. The time has come.

Together in the twenty-first century we can construct a unique way of life here, inspired by the traditions of Aboriginal Australia and of Europe and Asia. Land rights for Aboriginal Australians are in the best interests of all Australians. Land rights must respect the contributions made by those people who have immigrated here over the past two hundred years, as well as recognising the place of those who have always belonged to this land. That's what the Yothu Yindi balance means.

Two

INDIGENOUS MEDIA

Dot West

We sat in the river bed
Me mates and I,
We heard what you said
About our people, and oh what lies.

You spread your word
And images too,
Around the world
For all to view.

But one thing you forgot
Was the truth of the matter,
The forgotten lot
In a land of chatter.

You told of our fighting
Our drunk and roaming ways,
All the white sightings
Which only your eyes can portray.

You didn't know us
Or even understand,

When you took a guess
And reported, about the original inhabitants of
This land.

So back in that riverbed
We plotted and planned,
For our voice to be heard
In this racist land.

We're here now
With our own sound waves,
To tell of how
We became your slaves.

The stories are rich
And cultures strong,
We will teach
Of the right and the wrong.

So watch your voice
Young white one,
We now have a choice
To correct your tongue.

Non-indigenous Australians have held the power of the media for over 200 years, giving us various images of Australia including a negative portrayal of its indigenous population. We are now in a position to change the thinking of non-Aboriginal people and enlighten them as to who we are and what we do, and to take a look at the history of Australia from an Aboriginal point of view.

Looking at the history of Australia is certainly a learning process for non-Aboriginal people who have been educated from a white perspective. Just consider this point alone: when did you become aware that Aboriginal children were being taken away from their families and being raised in missions and institutions? And, more importantly, when did you find out how Aboriginal people felt about this genocidal treatment? I bet you didn't learn about it in your school books. We learnt about this along with the massacres, poisonings, rapes, the stealing of our country and many more sad and shameful crimes; we learnt it from our own people. We grew up with this history; our parents, grandparents, great-grandparents and even our great-great grandparents grew up knowing this history—we had to, we lived it, we are the victims of Australia's white history. Many of us had the opportunity to go to school and we did. But when school finished for the day we went home for an education about family, about land, about spirituality, about attitude, about respect. School was only part of our education.

So on our indigenous media outlets—on our radio stations, in our newspapers, in our books, on stage and through television—we tell our history, a history that white Australia cannot divorce itself from. But it's not all gloom and doom; we also tell of our rich and diverse culture, the relationship between the land and its people, of how the land and our people are one. We tell of our achievements in white society, our doctors, university graduates, medical and legal services, our writers, musicians and so on. But, most importantly, we tell of how we have survived, with our principles and culture intact.

The media have significant power to determine what issues are important and to set the public agenda. They have enormous power to shape the meaning of these issues and as a result can strongly influence peoples' ideas and values, including their ideas about Aboriginality. At their worst the media can help institutionalise racism. White Australians, like all white majorities, institutionalise their own value systems at the expense of minority groups. When white media portray us as savages, unemployed, drunks, criminals and just simply poor blacks, they are not only suppressing us as a people. They are reassuring themselves about their own race. Every time we're put down as savage or primitive or hopeless, white people are reassured that they are civilised, modern and successful. Aboriginal people are tired of being used as a sounding board for white society to bounce off ideas about its own identity.

We are also tired of being the subject of so much hypocritical scrutiny. There have been many times when I've seen non-Aboriginal people sitting in their glass houses getting sloshed to the eyeballs on alcohol and pointing their fingers and saying something like, 'Look at those black bludgers—they can't handle their grog'. This statement is racism at its worst and is often initiated and reflected by white media. The media tread carefully when it comes to white Australia's drinking problem, but there's no hesitation about stories to do with Aboriginal people and alcohol. Sometimes they're almost relished. We don't see the film crews go into white people's houses or the hotels, filming the drunken scenes and doing stories on the alcohol problems of whites. It's not done because the media would be telling white Australians that they're drunks. You might feel I'm getting into generalisation here, but that's exactly what the mainstream media does when they talk about the 'Aboriginal drinking problem'. That's nothing but a racist generalisation.

These media stereotypes do more than hurt the feelings and damage the aspirations of Aboriginal and Torres Strait Islander people. They are helping to build racist attitudes which I believe can cost lives. Look at the death in Perth of Louis Johnson. In January 1992, on his nineteenth birthday, Louis was deliberately driven over by white youths in a car. One of his killers later admitted this horrendous deed was committed because Louis was black.

But the threat to Louis' life was compounded when the ambulance officers decided to take this fatally injured boy home, rather than to hospital. They thought he was intoxicated and wanted to go home. He died a few hours later. At the inquest the head of the ambulance service said his officers had made an error of judgement that night. The issue of the ambulance officers' behaviour has not been legally resolved yet. At the inquest it was revealed that someone had written the word 'Abo' on Louis' patient report form. When the media stereotypes Aboriginal and Torres Strait Islander people as drunks and no-hopers and radical ratbags, they're helping build the racist attitudes that I believe led to Louis' death.

Racist attitudes towards Aboriginal people were being reinforced and circulated with great intensity in the Western Australian media in the lead up to the murder. From early 1990 the media presented juvenile delinquency and youth crime as having reached the proportions of a major social crisis. This appeared to coincide with the industrial and public relations interests of the police and was supported across the political spectrum. Most of the crimes (large or small) were directly attributed to young Aboriginal people, such that any youth-related crime in Western Australia is now almost automatically assumed to involve Aboriginal people.

The sensationalised treatment of juvenile crime, including car chases and the tragic deaths they caused, triggered public outcry, with tens of thousands of people marching to Parliament House demanding a judicial and police crack-down. The irresponsible reporting that led to this rally included comments like, 'Good riddance to bad rubbish, that's three less car thieves; I think they're dead, and I think that's good', by one radio personality on the death of three Aboriginal youths. It was startling that the murder of the Aboriginal youth Louis Johnson by *white* youths at the time did not rate the same sensational reporting or evoke the same outcry.

I'm not denying that many young Aboriginal people are in crisis; how could it be otherwise given their life circumstances? But I am questioning the grossly inflated news values given to youth offences. What good does this do, especially considering the difficulties in generating the same degree of popular emotion and community spirit to take action to resolve the social injustices suffered by indigenous people. What many Aboriginal people are critical of here is the day in, day out reporting by much of the news media. Far too often Australia's indigenous people are presented in a negative light and too seldom are our achievements reported.

But not all media treatment of Aboriginal affairs is negative and biased and we must recognise the good and conscientious work carried out by many journalists who have brought important issues to public attention and are working to raise the level of understanding. There are areas in which indigenous Australians have made gains and in which non-indigenous journalists have been eager to help. There are some examples that come to mind. The documentary 'Exile and the Kingdom', in which the people at Roebourne, Western Australia, tell their own story. The movie *Blackfellas* tells the story of a young Aboriginal man just out of prison trying to go straight, highlighting the many influences in his way. The music industry's embrace of the talent of Yothu Yindi is another example, and the national simulcast of *Stompem Ground 1992*, the Kimberley Aboriginal Arts and Cultural Festival, certainly demonstrated our musical talents. The National Media and Indigenous Peoples conference held earlier this year gave us all hope as the media recognised they have made blunders and will look to improve their reporting about Australia's indigenous people.

Just as mainstream media can change attitudes so can Aboriginal and Torres Strait Islander media. As an example I'll tell you the story of a Kimberley group which commenced its first broadcast in 1987 on the ABC. The Aboriginal community wanted a way to help maintain their own languages, and portray and inform about their own culture and way of life. They also wanted to counteract the bad publicity their people were receiving in the local paper and the consequent low self-esteem the local Aboriginal people felt when they dealt with the white community. Interestingly enough, when this group first started broadcasting it was the only media group apart from the ABC providing a radio service to this region. So the audience was not only the Aboriginal people but also the non-Aboriginal community. They were able to target the whole community and some attitudes certainly changed during this time. You see, this group didn't just turn white people's thinking about, it also turned the thinking of the Aboriginal community. It made people proud to be Aboriginal in the white-dominated community. Over time the service empowered a group of people who once felt powerless in their own country. It instilled pride and built self-esteem amongst the young and old. Here was an Aboriginal organisation providing an essential service not only to its own community but also to the wider community. The broadcasts were for everyone.

This is just one example in the very short time Aboriginal and Torres Strait Islander people have been involved in the media industry. We now have six Aboriginal radio stations licensed, about another six groups working towards a licence, about ninety remote communities licensed to deliver both radio and television services, various newspapers, a television station, many performers in all fields of the arts, authors, playwriters, a publishing house and the list goes on. It all just demonstrates the natural ability of the people and the motivation and drive to be seen, heard and accepted for what we are. No longer can we be portrayed in white media from only a white perspective. We're telling our own stories.

Our role in the media industry is not just to inform our own people but also to educate and inform non-Aboriginal people. We report on the news and current affairs which are relevant to our people, we tell of what's going on in the languages of our area or in a more easily understood form of English. We try to cut out what we call high English, which is where big words are used. High English is used by mainstream media and more often than not we need the English dictionary at hand to work out what is actually being said, but then so does most of white Australia. Down to earth language is all that is needed. We are not out to impress people, we are out to inform, to communicate. With high English it's more than likely you will fail to communicate. For example we don't say 'legislation' when 'law' will do.

Indigenous media in Australia have a big role in maintaining our languages. At the time of invasion there were about 250 different Aboriginal and Torres Strait Islander languages, there are now fewer than ninety still in use, and not all of them are spoken as first languages. The loss of many of Australia's indigenous languages is hardly surprising. Many of our grandparents were forbidden to speak their language as young people when they were pushed into missions or into settlements to be assimilated into white culture. The languages were not passed on to their children and their children's children. The media have to bear some of the blame for the loss of Australia's indigenous languages. Just think of the impact it would have on white Australians if they were fed only Aboriginal and Islander languages through the radio, on TV and in the newspapers for over 200 years. The English language would no doubt be dead by now. But many of ours survived and we as indigenous people and you as white Australians have a responsibility to enhance, nurture and maintain as many of our languages as possible.

There's a funny story I heard about from one region where an Aboriginal media group was taking the national news to our people in the local Aboriginal languages so our people could understand fully what was happening in the world. There was an uproar from the white community. They were basically paranoid because they didn't understand what was being said and felt that we were plotting against them or planning something dreadful. They just didn't understand that our communities couldn't fathom their words either and needed them interpreted.

The government directly funds two national media services, the Special Broadcasting Service which is to reflect Australia's multicultural society and the Australian Broadcasting Corporation which is to provide an independent service. Both are to entertain, inform and educate all Australians. It's really ironic when you think that these media services have been provided by government, while there's a lack of long term planning to cater to Aboriginal and Torres Strait Islanders and the indigenous media service. It is widely believed by many indigenous Australians that the ABC caters to non-indigenous Australians and SBS caters to the ethnic population. Admittedly both services have provided very good programs for and about Aboriginal and Torres Strait Islander people, but it hasn't been often enough, nor localised enough. The SBS ensures that immigrants to this country are able to maintain and broadcast their own languages and inform Australia about their culture. This alone was certainly a credit to the Federal Government for its insight and appreciation of other cultures, but once again it forgot the diverse needs of its own indigenous culture.

The population of Australia's Aboriginal and Torres Strait Islander community is extremely diverse in its culture with many different languages spoken. Think of the Kimberley region of Western Australia, roughly the size of Victoria and Tasmania combined: if you travel through the Kimberley with its large Aboriginal population and the diversity of the people within this region, it's just like travelling through Europe with its changing cultures and languages. So can you imagine these national media groups trying to service Australia's indigenous people? Of course SBS and the ABC have their own charters to provide programs for and about Australia's indigenous people, but it would be extremely naive to think that this alone would meet our needs. SBS's task is made even more difficult since their programs are only broadcast in the capital cities.

The ABC realised it couldn't cater to all of our people. In 1981 after consultation the Corporation began to allow different Aboriginal media groups to have access to the ABC's radio airwaves. This arrangement commenced in 1981/2 when the ABC purchased radio programs from CAAMA, the Central Australian Aboriginal Media Association of Australia, and then broadcast them under ABC control. In 1985 the first unsupervised access on the ABC was undertaken by the

Torres Strait Islanders and in the same year Aboriginal people in Perth were broadcasting on the ABC. In 1987 and 1988 Aboriginal access extended to the Kimberley region where groups could broadcast within their own regions and in their own languages. This arrangement was not met very favourably by some bureaucrats. One senior officer even expressed concern about having foreign languages go to air on a national broadcast transmitter! However, this attitude didn't prevail. There are now three radio stations in the Kimberley producing and presenting about thirty-five hours of Aboriginal programs to the region via the ABC.

Australians were experimenting with radio as far back as 1905, and the first station, 2SB in Sydney, began broadcasting in November 1923. But it wasn't until June 1976 when Melbourne's station 3CR broadcast the country's first Aboriginal radio program. One month later 2XX in Canberra transmitted Australia's second Aboriginal radio show. So it took fifty-three years for our voice to be heard in our own programs, and this came about initially through the Public and community radio stations which only started operating in the mid seventies. There are now over 100 licensed community radio stations and about thirty of them have some Aboriginal and Torres Strait Islander programs. These include six stations owned and operated by Aboriginal and Torres Strait Islander media organisations in Alice Springs, Brisbane, Townsville, Port Augusta, Perth and Kununurra.

We now have over 500 hours a week of indigenous radio being produced by indigenous people. If you consider the short amount of time we've been involved and the lack of clear policy and direction from government to cater to our growing needs, you will realise we have achieved against all odds and are still doing so. Unfortunately, TV presents a different story. Less than one per cent of Australia's television programs are produced by indigenous people.

We have been able to apply our talents to the media industry like a duck takes to water. Many indigenous media workers have developed great broadcasting and production skills with very little or no formal training at all. But the indigenous media industry feels it is essential to provide training opportunities for our people in this field of work, not only tertiary education but also practical training in all areas of the industry from management and journalism to technical skills. There still needs to be a more concentrated effort made to increase the numbers and ensure that all positions within our own organisations are occupied by indigenous people.

The media industry has opened up greater employment and training opportunities for skilling our people. It is estimated that over 200 Aboriginal and Torres Strait Islander people are involved in community media either as employed staff or volunteers. The ABC currently employs seventy-three and SBS sixteen indigenous Australians in various fields of their operations. But you can count on one hand the number of Aboriginal and Torres Strait Islanders employed in the commercial electronic media, and the numbers for the print media are even lower. This might improve shortly as the Federal Government through the Royal Commission into Aboriginal Deaths in Custody is providing money for these specific industries to train and employ more indigenous people.

How the Government has handled some of the recommendations from the Royal Commission is a prime example of how low on the priority list indigenous media is. Recommendation 205 was split into two parts, the first part emphasising the importance of indigenous media and recommending further funding where necessary, while the second part stressed the need for Aboriginal and Torres Strait Islander people to be employed in mainstream media and this media to set up codes of practice for use when reporting about indigenous Australians. The Federal Government has provided funds to mainstream media to train indigenous people and has also funded a national meeting to address the codes of practice issue. But on the other hand the indigenous media industry is still struggling for adequate funding, and some organisations have been operating on the smell of an oily rag. To this date no money has been provided to indigenous media from the Deaths in Custody funding. It appears that white industry once again has claimed black dollars.

Even when money has been spent in our communities, it has often been a case of one step forward and two steps back.

In early 1984 the Federal Government formed a special task force to advise on Aboriginal broadcasting and telecommunications policies. The Task Force report, 'Out of the Silent Land', was released later that year and in 1985 the Government endorsed over fifty of its recommendations. 'Out of the Silent Land' addressed the lack of telecommunications and electronic media available to Aboriginal people living in remote Australia. Several very important issues were raised in this report which then mapped out the development of indigenous media for the next eight years. Firstly the report placed a high emphasis on the need to develop indigenous media within remote Australia, at the same time stating that city-based broadcasting was being catered for through the public broadcasting sector. Sadly this report did not go far enough to cater to the growing needs of indigenous media, and the eight years were stifling for many groups.

The report also highlighted the need to offset the impact of western television and radio in remote communities, which was brought about by the launch of AUSSAT's first generation of satellites. In the year of the bicentennial some eighty-five remote Aboriginal and Torrest Strait Islander communities were given, through the Department of Aboriginal Affairs, a facility called BRACS, Broadcasting for Remote Aboriginal Communities Scheme. The package included a satellite dish and decoder along with some basic equipment which allowed the community to interrupt the radio or television signal and broadcast their own programs within a five kilometre radius. Brilliant idea, fantastic plan, but what was forgotten were three very important factors for the system's success: consultation, training and on-going funding. In many of the eighty-five communities who received BRACS, there was no consultation by the Department of Aboriginal Affairs about whether they wanted the equipment or not. It was just delivered and installed. Many of these communities say that they were given only a half hour course in how to operate the equipment. They were shown how to receive the station of their choice, how to turn the machinery off and on and that really it wasn't until about a year later when the bureaucrats got it together enough to realise training programs were necessary to teach the community members how to interrupt the incoming signal and to make and present their own community-based programs. People needed to be taught how to operate a video camera, produce and present their own radio and television programs, and how to interview and edit. But in most cases it wasn't until two years after the installation of BRACS that people received this training.

In the meantime the communities had become accustomed to the daily soapies and the general infilitration of western culture. As an Aboriginal person you start to wonder about the motivation behind BRACS and the Government's failure to meet the challenge it supposedly set itself: to allow remote Aboriginal and Islander communities to interrupt the broadcasting of western civilisation to their communities. Was the delay in providing training and infrastructure a subconscious infiltration of white society into Australia's indigenous communities? It certainly appeared that way.

Now that we have ATSIC, the Aboriginal and Torres Strait Islander Commission, things are looking up for the remote communities. Just this year the Commissioners realised the worth of indigenous media and the importance of BRACS. In their new policy paper they have said they will develop a detailed strategy for the revitalisation, over the next three years, of BRACS. In the first year they plan to pump one million dollars into the revitalisation and another quarter of a million into training.

It is important that we not see BRACS as a total failure. Despite the way it arrived, it has been put to excellent use by a number of communities. Even though BRACS has been installed in communities for a number of years without clear government policy or assistance, in many parts of Australia BRACS local programming is part of many communities' daily life. It has been used to bail up visiting government officials and put them on the spot in front of a camera. This then allows community members who don't attend the council meetings an insight as to who's visiting, and why. The remote broadcasting scheme is used extensively to inform the community of the daily business of council and its workers. Cultural events are also a big highlight. The community schools can access the service and broadcast their own programs and learn about electronic media. But there are still a lot of communities which don't do local programming and allow the satellite feed to just keep broadcasting white media. Soapies such as 'Days of Our Lives' keep spilling into remote Australia. With appropriate funding and assistance this situation will no doubt change very shortly, when the communities have the power and training to decide about the use of BRACS and the direction they want to take.

Setting up our media groups around Australia has been hard work, especially in the absence of progressive policy for indigenous media. But that hasn't been our only problem; we've had to convince our own people and the major funding bodies that indigenous media is a priority, and not just a luxury. We've had to compete for limited funds. While issues like health and education are clearly important priorities, we've argued that indigenous media can help to tackle these issues by raising people's awareness and morale.

The Department of Aboriginal and Islander Affairs began a policy development process back in 1987 which resulted in many draft reports being written but never made public, unless of course they fell off the back of a truck, which many did. Indigenous media workers along with their communities became extremely frustrated when reports were not produced even though the consultation process, in an ad hoc fashion, had been conducted. We've been waiting for the promised new policy for over five years now. It has been extremely hard for the broadcasting sector within the Department of Aboriginal and Torres Strait Islander Affairs to attract extra money without a clear policy. There was only a small number of Aboriginal and Torres Strait Islander media groups fortunate enough to get on the funding list of the then Department of Aboriginal Affairs. The rest were left to fend for themselves or try for the small amount of funding available for Aboriginal broadcasting in the Public broadcasting sector. In some cases the funding arrangements were a matter of who screamed the loudest and knocked at the Department's door the longest. This was no way to develop an industry.

It was not until 1991, nearly seventy years after the birth of Australian radio, that the Aboriginal and Torres Strait Islander Commission along with the Department of Transport and Communication wrote a discussion paper about Aboriginal and Torres Strait Islander broadcasting policy. It became a long and bureaucratic process but eventually in April 1993 after much consultation the Commissioners of ATSIC endorsed a new policy paper for indigenous media in Australia.

To a certain extent the new policy is reflective of what is happening within Aboriginal and Torres Strait Islander broadcasting and what will be developed in the future. However, there are still some areas of concern. The major one is the use of the word 'broadcasting' when, in actual fact, we in the industry also include our newspaper outlets, but the policy paper doesn't recognise this form of media. There are other areas of concern but it is apparent that ATSIC plans to use the newly formed National Indigenous Media Association as a body to consult with and receive advice from. We as the indigenous media industry now have a forum for negotiations.

There is one other important aspect of this new paper, a long term goal: in association with Aboriginal and Torres Strait Islander broadcasters ATSIC will seek recognition and appropriate funding of the indigenous broadcasting sector in its own right within the framework of the Government's mainstream broadcasting structure. If this goal is implemented it will mean that we will be competing for funds with the rest of the broadcasting sector of Australia such as the ABC and SBS and it will also allow our industry to have the same recognition and importance as our national broadcasters.

Until that recommendation is implemented media organisations that receive ATSIC grants face a conflict of interest. Our communities expect us to report truthfully and fairly. But in some instances it becomes extremely difficult for this to happen in relation to ATSIC, our funding body. If there is an adverse story about a regional council or councillor we're potentially compromised since these same people decide on our organisations' funding.

As indigenous media groups we have operated for many years in separate arenas. There were the groups who received DAA/ATSIC funding, and the groups who broadcast on public radio; others who broadcast on the ABC; the print media; the television and video production groups and not forgetting our individual indigenous media workers in the ABC and the SBS. We all knew that we wanted to form a national body to include all indigenous media groups and people as a forum to assist the struggle and endeavours of our community within this industry. In May of 1992 a meeting was held in Canberra which formed the national body on an interim basis and in May 1993 the National Indigenous Media Association of Australia held its inaugural annual general meeting. The association's major objective is to represent indigenous media groups individually and collectively on a local, state, national and international basis while maintaining and respecting the uniqueness and authority of every group. As a collective of all indigenous media in Australia we want to enhance and further develop the industry nationally and assist communities in the establishment, operating and development of their own media.

Like many of my fellow workers I have hopes for the future in relation to indigenous media in Australia. I don't think my vision is very different from that of other people. I would like Australia to recognise there is an indigenous media sector which does exist and has existed and developed for many years. A national indigenous network is the logical next step. The service should have the capacity not only to be televised from a capital city, but also to broadcast nationally from a region such as the Kimberley. We need to provide local services like BRACS, and enable communities to intercept the national broadcast and televise their own local programs. That local service would be crucial in recognising our cultural diversity and the language differences within Australia's indigenous nation. The same approach could also apply to radio.

Non-indigenous Australians could benefit enormously from a strong indigenous media service. You would not only get a better informed view about our culture but also you'd be able to see pictures of yourselves from another point of view. Whites have made plenty of documentaries about our people; what about Aboriginal people making a series of documentaries about white suburbia? What about Aboriginal comedy and soapies? I'm sure you as white Australians are sick of seeing and hearing all the political and contentious issues surrounding us, but there's a lot more to life and we can share this with you.

Everyone in Australia could benefit from such a media service which would give a more truthful and positive view about ourselves as indigenous Australians. Perhaps with such a service it would make it harder for another racist murder such as Louis Johnson's to happen again. The possibilities for our future development are endless but we can't do it without community and government support. After all, we are an essential service and we see ourselves as providers of a service for all Australians, a service that reflects the cultural diversity of this country.

White Australia is now becoming aware that there is a black Australia and, more importantly, is starting to appreciate us as a people and feel proud of this country's indigenous culture. This alone is an important achievement, but we do need to reflect this culture more within our media by portraying indigenous life in all its diversity. With this a greater understanding and awareness will evolve and a healthier Australia will emerge.

I will end with these words from a poem of Jack Davis:

> Let these two worlds combine,
> Yours and mine.
> The door between us is not locked,
> Just ajar.

Three

TOWARDS A KOORI HEALING PRACTICE

Ian Anderson

On 11 June 1987 Arthur Moffat, a 51-year-old Aboriginal man, was found dead in a cell in the Warragul Police Station. He had been taken to the police station from the platform of the railway station, having been removed thereto from a train on which he had been travelling. Everything done to Arthur Moffat—the removal from the train, the placing on the railway platform, the removal to the police station and the detention in the cells—was based on the assumption that he was simply intoxicated. The only basis for this assumption was that he smelt of alcohol, was only partly conscious, and was an Aboriginal. The police called ambulance officers to the police station who confirmed this assumption.

The assumption was unsound. Arthur Moffat was most probably suffering a hypoglycaemic reaction due to the combination of diabetes, heavy drinking and not eating. Very simple attention could have saved his life.

(Wootten, 1990: 1)[1]

The police and ambulance officers who were a part of this series of errors should have known that the assumptions under which they were operating were unsound. In the case of the police their actions were directly contrary to the spirit of their standing orders. This is not a matter of a single incorrect diagnosis. It was a series of social interactions in which police and ambulance officers made dubious assumptions. On every occasion they confirmed each other's judgement. I doubt those involved would have been so certain about their judgement if Arthur Moffat was not an Aboriginal man left semi-comatose on a country railway station. If Arthur Moffat had been dressed in a business suit and found on the steps of the stock exchange he would very likely be alive today.

Arthur Moffat, like ten percent of the adult Aboriginal community, was diabetic. Knowing this problem is very common in the Aboriginal community may have saved this man's life. Yet all involved presumed a semi-conscious Aboriginal man was a mere drunk. So that it is unlikely that technical knowledge alone about Aboriginal diabetes would have altered the behaviour of the police and ambulance officers. Their behaviour only makes sense by reference to particular racist stereotypes of Aboriginality.

These stereotypes have their own logic, having grown out of the social relations between Aboriginal people and non-Aboriginal people on the colonial frontier. This coloured lens of white colonial heritage represents Aborigines as naive primitives unable to handle the dangerous moral products of civilisation such as the grog.

In the south-east, where I live, most interactions between Koories and non-Aboriginal people are fleeting. So when encounters do occur people often resort to those colonial images, and act accordingly. I see this encounter between an Aboriginal man and the health and custodial systems as entrenched in the broader context of relations between Aboriginal and non-Aboriginal Australia. Experienced, skilled workers do make mistakes of this order when dealing with Koori people—not only because they lack technical knowledge, but because their actions continue to be driven by a colonial view of Aboriginal Australia.

The case of Arthur Moffat raises a series of problems

about medical practice and Koori people.[2] Firstly, how do the submerged assumptions and biases of medical practitioners colour the perception of Aboriginal people and consequently shape their diagnosis and treatment of Koori ill-health? Following on from this, how do the experiences of Koori people shape their encounters with medicine? I am deeply concerned about the persistence of tragedies such as Arthur Moffat's death. Yet I also feel we need to aim for more than disaster prevention. We must take heed of these experiences, and prevent them being repeated. But we also need to move beyond them, to realise the powerful potential of a healing practice based on Koori values—a truly Aboriginal approach to health care.

Just as our existing Aboriginal health services helped to open new ground in community health, I believe we can lead the way again, with a healing practice based on Koori ideas of well-being. But we can only do this if we accept that Aboriginal people's experience of medicine is part of a history which includes invasion and on-going colonisation. This colonial process has dis-empowered people, controlling their intellectual life, taking from them their right to organise their collective life. An anti-colonial project like this must empower Koori people by acknowledging their experience of medicine, and their understanding of health issues.

I don't consider my knowledge of Koori health issues to be an 'expertise'. The academic tradition creates so-called truths about health and healing which are accessible to only the specialist few. I consider my knowledge to be a product of my own particular experiences, certainly in professional training, but equally in being a part of and working within the Koori community.

In an education system which deifies textual knowledge, other ways of knowing or learning get poor recognition. It sometimes seems as if intellectual activity develops in a social or experiential vacuum—a kind of divine inspiration. That's not the case. So I want to acknowledge, and pay respect to, those individuals who have been (and continue to be) my teachers within my own community. Their experiences and knowledge have been influential in shaping my understanding of the issues in Aboriginal health.

This approach has two implications. First, it means I am speaking *from* the experience of being Koori. I am not speaking *for* indigenous Australian communities in general. I can't speak for Murris, Nungas, Noongars, Yolngu, Anangu or any other Aboriginal or Islander mob. Second, in speaking from a Koori experience, I am well aware of the common prejudice that we Aboriginal people in the south-east have lost our culture as well as our land. I don't accept this. I am quite passionately committed to working within what I see as being a Koori tradition.

Working as a doctor within my sense of the values or practices of Koori tradition, I need a framework for thinking critically about medical work in Koori communities. I need to consider the extent to which the practice of western-derived medicine is counter to the empowerment of Aboriginal people, and the Aboriginalisation of health care. For me, this understanding is the outcome of a commitment to working with Koori communities who seek to redefine medical work in order to better service their own mob.

An alternative healing practice may remain centred on the needs of the Koori body, but it has to comprehend the body holistically. I see the Koori body as much more than an interconnected system of muscles, bone or fat. The bodies which we inhabit also have cultural and social dimensions. In fact the cultured nature of our experience of bodies is such that even the so-called objective body of clinical science is in itself a culturally shaped perception of the body.

Medicine doesn't operate only in the realm of organic disease. Healing practices also impact on the development of a sense of self, and on how you value your body. Illnesses such as diabetes, even though they may eventually threaten life or result in debilitating complications, often have minimal symptoms in the short term. For many Koories, looking after their diabetes is embedded within other needs and experiences, like finding work, finding suitable housing and getting a useful education.

I want to see a form of healing practice which constructively engages with all those processes which contribute to the development of Koori well-being, rather than one which is only concerned with bugs and tumours and suchlike. This is obviously an ambitious project. In a moment I want to lay out some of the ground-work, by outlining the important issues which underlie such a transformation. We can realise the visionary potential of Koori health by thinking with our hearts, but with one eye on the past and one towards the future.

The Aboriginal Health Services

Before I talk about a future Koori health care practice, let's consider the history that makes these questions possible. The community-controlled Aboriginal Health Services emerged at a key moment in the history of the Aboriginal political movement. Until the 1960s, Aboriginal political activity was essentially a civil rights movement, concerned with issues like citizenship and equal pay. When the 1967 referendum removed the constitutional barriers to Aboriginal citizenship, Aboriginal politics was transformed. Ideas of autonomy, self-determination and sovereignty became central to the new political terrain. The new attitude was crystallised by the words of Kevin Gilbert: *Because a White Man'll Never Do It.*[3] Koories, frustrated with continuing poor access to health services, were convinced the Aboriginal community had to take into its own hands the responsibility for delivering its health services. In this new era the key issue became how Koories would exercise their rights to health care.

Koories have had good reason for anger with the inadequacies of the mainstream health system. Prior to the development of the Aboriginal health services, access to any form of health care service could not be guaranteed. The most significant barrier to health care was poverty, and the indifference, even frank hostility, of some health care providers. Stories like Arthur Moffat's were all too common in those days.

Aboriginal people were only able to interact at the margins of the system—and then often with difficulty. The Koori experience was to be treated on the hospital verandah, or having to 'trouble' a resentful private practitioner. In the 1960s, The Victorian Aborigines Welfare Board[4] wrote to medical practitioners in Victoria requesting information on the health of Victorian Aborigines. One doctor replied in 1966 that:

> I do think of them as 'pests' by and large because the 5% of [A]boriginal patients would account for perhaps 50% of late night calls and week-end work ... In my earlier days here, I would sometimes try to collect a fee, particularly if a group arrived in a taxi from 40 miles away, but now do not—it upsets me—not them ...
>
> I resent them for this double imposition—this is a busy practice and sleep can be precious and I get very little time to spend with my family of five ...[5]

This doctor thought of his patients as pests, so it is likely that they were treated as such. Koories were resented for intruding into his private time. We may sympathise with someone whose family life suffers because of his work. But his patronising attitude is inexcusable and it betrays a complete lack of understanding of how the conditions of Koori life shaped their encounters with medicine.

It's attitudes like this that promoted the very problem he's complaining about. Knowing they would be unwelcome pests, Koories were hardly likely to make an appointment for a routine check-up. They were far more likely to wait until they needed urgent care, possibly late at night and certainly far sicker than they needed to be. In the design and delivery of health services Koories were perceived and treated as if they were outside of the health system. They were seen as an unnecessary burden, rather than people who were the entitled recipients of health care.

Coinciding with the growth of a vigorous Aboriginal health movement there was also a shift in the relationship between the Australian state and Aboriginal people. After decades of imagining itself as a dominion of the British empire, the Australian nation awoke from its post-World War Two slumber to find such an attitude was no longer possible. In this context the policies and practices of Aboriginal assimilation became increasingly untenable. They merged into the more pluralistic policy model of welfare colonialism.

Unlike the older idea of nationhood, it was now possible to be Aboriginal and be considered a part of the Australian community. In place of the old Protection Boards and their mission managers we now have a large bureaucracy which administers Aboriginal programs. The political activities of the Aboriginal health movement managed to drive a wedge into the space opened by this shift in colonial relations. One outcome of this wedge of conflict was the Aboriginal health services.

These health services were created by the community to be controlled by the community. They operate under an elected community board of management. This organisational structure gives Koories the opportunity to design and deliver health programs for their own people, and to develop health policy and strategies. Aboriginal health workers collaborate with largely non-Aboriginal practitioners such as doctors, nurses and dentists. Koori people are able to choose staff who they judge will work as their advocates, and demonstrate respect for their culture.

By creating these centres the Aboriginal health movement has created Aboriginal places where health care services can be delivered. Koori communities have defined through collaboration and dispute how the health services should be administered, how accountability should be ensured, and how work roles should be defined. The services have worked hard to ensure that individuals working in Aboriginal communities operate within the parameters set down by the community.

I don't wish to naively idealise these services. But they have created primary health centres where Koories can comfortably go, see a Koori health worker, and be treated with respect by people who know something of their lives and culture. But the doctor they see will most likely be non-Aboriginal and working with an often inappropriate bio-medical model of health. This is about more than whether or not individual practitioners are sensitive to individual and community experience. We need to develop a new form of practice which we can use to better realise the visions of Koori people.

Koories and Medicine

To tackle the problems of the relationship between Koories and the institution of medicine, we need to examine the social context of medical practice. One of the key factors which enabled the profession of medicine to develop its dominant position within the health system was an alliance, albeit an often troubled one, between the state and medicine. Medicine has, for example, the power to certify absence from work, and regulate access to a vast number of pharmaceutical and other therapeutic substances.

More fundamentally medical practice is premised on people consenting to change their life practices to take medication as directed, present for surgery or perhaps change their diet. In this form of practice, relief from suffering depends on the patient submitting to medical authority. By intervening in people's life practices at the moment of actual or potential harm medicine transforms our bodies. It does this by imposing particular values on how we should be or behave.

The medical knowledge of the body conveys a claim to 'truth', that the doctor knows your body better than you ever will. This scientific knowledge of the body has its cultural origins in the late eighteenth century development of the clinic. Within the clinic it became possible to investigate and examine bodies and locate diseases in particular sites within the emerging cultural construct of the scientific body.

In the twentieth century, with the development of sophisticated mechanisms of population surveillance and new research methodologies, this terrain has extended to include not only actual disease, but also potential disease. The emphasis within contemporary medicine on prevention is founded on the notion that risk, like actual illness, can be managed by changing lifestyle.

So according to this perception, diabetes is an abnormality in the regulation of blood glucose which has particular effects on organs such as the heart, kidney and eyes. Medicine can intervene once the disease occurs in order to alleviate sickness. Alternatively, diabetes may be prevented by adopting particular dietary or exercise practices. Both in its broader social context, but also in the day-to-day relationships between doctors and patients, medicine has the power to very literally regulate or shape people's lives. This power depends on the medical perception of the body.

Good outcomes are of course possible. But it does depend on whether patients and doctors agree on strategies of care. For the patients such interventions must be economically and socially possible **and** desirable. This can be difficult enough when patients and doctors share a class and cultural background. You can imagine how much more difficult it is if the advice is being given by a member of a colonising culture to a member of a colonised one.

When doctors talk about how patients respond to intervention and instruction, they talk about compliance. And it's not unusual to hear doctors voice concern of 'poor compliance' among Koori patients. This is important because the extent to which a patient is seen to comply sometimes decides their access to health care. For Koories, well-being as a value has as much to do with family relationships as it has to do with their experience of their physical body.

A Koori person with kidney failure who is treated with dialysis may find their commitments to their kidneys conflicting with the needs of their family. It's sometimes difficult to respond to the demands of an extended family with limited resources, *and* balance this with a strict regime of dialysis. In cutting dialysis time, the Koori patients aren't necessarily neglecting their own well-being. They are operating within the framework of Koori notions of well-being. Doctors may view such patients as poorly motivated or insufficiently compliant.[6] A patient deemed to be poorly motivated risks being judged as undeserving of costly resources such as transplant services. In this regard medical practitioners are brokers—they regulate access to particular resources. The so-called better patients may indeed have better access to more specialised and costly resources.

My point is, medical interventions are not value free, and doctors are powerfully positioned to transform the lives of their patients. These transformations are not limited to the organic realm. Medicine is as an agent of cultural change. It seeks to relieve suffering by modifying how people act and how they think. This process has profound implications for who Koories are and how Koories imagine themselves to be. In a moral sense this is neither necessarily good nor bad. Healing practices of any kind have such implications. However, Koories are entitled to a healing practice which bears out our vision of ourselves, and not one which reinforces the coercion and the helplessness of colonial stereotypes. This problem is integral to the operation of clinical medicine, regardless of where it's practised.

In thinking about the practice of medicine this way I'm not saying anything particularly new. Neither am I debunking the need for this type of healing. However, I am committed to the idea of a Koori healing practice which maintains the benefits of a biomedical practice, but takes the implication of these criticisms seriously.

Koori Healing Practices

This is not just a clinical or intellectual problem, it is also a matter of imagination. The doctor in the clinic needs to consider that their interpretation of patient experience is as subjective as it is objective. A Koori healing practice would require a more disciplined form of imagination in order to better understand how someone comes to call on health service resources. People seek health resources because of the experience of their body. This experience has a number of inextricably linked aspects—there's the interpretation of body senses, interaction with other people through time, and a history of prior encounters with the health system. The body which enters the clinic is a product of organic and social processes which are so intertwined it's impossible to engage with, or intervene in, either realm without impacting on the other.

The Koori body develops and transforms in a particular set of personal historical and social circumstances. For Koories, important aspects of this growth are the experience of an extending kinship system and an experience of non-Aboriginal institutions and society. Through the process of development certain values become embodied. For example, our concept of well-being is not only an idea which we use to assess body experience, it also drives our body in particular ways. This transforming experience of who I am and how I experience my body, as a Koori, is a key dynamic. It shapes how people come to the health system and, following each encounter, it continues to give form to their behaviour.

So Aunty's experience of a diabetic leg ulcer isn't just an experience of pain or discomfort. It also incorporates the difficulties she has in meeting family needs, getting the transport or money to see a doctor, and the humiliation she feels when the doctor berates her for not looking after herself.

The impact this might have on the clinical interaction can be realised if practitioners look beyond the body parts made available to them by the coloured lens of clinical science. They need to engage with the other abstract forms bodies can take. Healing is not only an empirical science. It is not just a question of choosing the appropriate treatment. By giving a name and conferring meaning to the patient's problem, the doctor takes the first step in narrowing the range of solutions available to the patient. To do this constructively in a Koori healing practice we need a new form of medical imagination. This is possible if we take into account how the overlaying dynamics of the doctor/patient and the Koori/non-Aboriginal relationship shape the perception of the Koori body. Certainly this would have helped Arthur Moffat. Likewise, it may cause some doctors to question their ability to judge a Koori patient as poorly motivated.

Some aspects of the embodied experience of Koories in the clinical encounter are simply beyond, or incommensurate with, standard medical practice. The Koori Aunt with diabetes who lives in an overcrowded inadequate house and has considerable difficulty in achieving good diabetic control, has a body which bears the experience of poor housing. In cramped and inadequate living conditions, the need to negotiate a diabetic diet is likely to be one of many unnecessary stresses. Even though Aunty may say she wants to maintain good diabetic control, her will may not be sufficient when a feed of fast food is both the one and only treat for the day and keeps a mob of kids' bellies quiet.

Now it's a difficult argument to sustain, using the logic of a rational clinical science, that Aunty's poor housing causes her diabetes to be unmanageable. However, if we take into account all the possible dimensions of her embodied experience we might be able to develop strategies which would not be made apparent by scientific reasoning alone.

Finding better housing for Aunty might achieve better control of her diabetes. With a few less mouths to feed in the one household it would be easier for her to negotiate her diet.

Koori life experience and medical practice are not diametrically opposed. There is basis for interaction. They have much in common, such as a concern for control of pain or the alleviation of suffering. However, the skills required in getting consensus on such concerns are not intuitive. Nor are they necessarily facilitated by traditional modes of clinical interaction.

Understanding the relationship between Koories and medical practice has certain profound implications. Firstly, the set of conditions which shape these encounters such as the experience of poverty, poor housing conditions or conflicting values of well-being, can't be viewed simply as constraints on medical practice. It's not good enough for doctors to maintain the attitude, 'given an ideal world what we would do is ...'

Rather, these so-called constraints on medical intervention must be understood as integral to the practice of healing. So for the diabetic Koori living in an inadequate house, getting reasonable housing is as integral to the problem of diabetes as is the choice of medication. Doctors must see that the extent to which people incorporate medical advice is not the responsibility of the patient alone. It's a problem of the doctor-patient relationship.

A new Koori healing practice would recognise that historically medicine has been poorly attuned to Koori values of well-being and the conditions which have shaped this. We would need to move beyond the traditional encounter between one doctor and one patient. We have to find new forms of interaction between doctors and patients and other staff such as Aboriginal health workers. This would shift our focus from the diagnosis and treatment of disease. It would enable patients to actively engage in negotiating their problems and their healing strategies. This reorientation takes the health care provider out of the individual client-practitioner consultation into the social realm in which the patient's well-being develops.

The dynamics of families and communities are fundamental to a Koori vision of well-being. So only focussing on Aunty's blood sugar readings will miss some of the most important influences on Aunty's well-being. Is Aunty's dietary change only to be achieved by persistently telling her how to eat better? How might our strategies change if we focussed on the family and not the individual? We could even go beyond that and develop strategies for community healing.

Until recently few people in the broader community cared if medical practitioners considered Aboriginal patients pests. Over the last two decades some sections of the health bureaucracy have demonstrated some interest, often after considerable political debate, in improving their performance on Koori health issues. But in the politics of Aboriginal health, the institution of medicine has been somewhat more peripherally involved. Academic centres and professional bodies have taken up issues of Aboriginal health, but to date they have had a secondary role in the development of Aboriginal health services.

The death of Arthur Moffat was a tragedy. Yet on a daily basis this tragedy is re-enacted, albeit in a more mundane way. Changing the relationship between medicine and Koori communities is more than removing the veneer of bigoted language. It requires us to question the very values inherent in medical practice. This requires an ongoing cultural activism, questioning the cultural basis of medical practice. Such activism takes the struggle for better health services into the academy where medical knowledge and medical practitioners are made.

1 Wootten, J H (Commissioner) (1990): *Report of the Inquiry into the Death of Arthur Moffatt* Royal Commission Into Aboriginal Deaths in Custody, Canberra, Australian Government Publishing Service

2 My intention is to focus my remarks on the aspect of health care work which I am primarily, but not exclusively involved in. Medicine has a particular position within a larger occupational field of health services which adds another dimension to the issues which I will discuss.

3 Gilbert, Kevin J (1973): *Because a White Man'll Never Do It*, Sydney, Angus and Robertson

4 The Aborigines Welfare Board was created under the Aborigines Act with the function to 'promote the moral, intellectual and physical welfare of [A]borigines ... with a view to their assimilation into the general community' (Lyons, G (1983): 'Official Policy Toward Victorian Aborigines 1957–1974', *Aboriginal History*, 7, 61–81).

5 From documents in the author's possession

6 Anderson, Ian (1992): 'Access, equity and the ethics of resource allocation for minority groups: A Koori perspective' in *Choice or Chance? The Ethics of Resource Allocation for Minority Groups: Ethics of Resource Allocation in Health Discussion Paper 3* Australian Health Ethics Committee.

Four

AUSTRALIA'S INDIGENOUS LANGUAGES

Jeanie Bell

I was born in Brisbane at a time when Murries were being pushed off reserves. Both of my parents had lived on government settlements and had been sent there in much earlier days as children, when the policy was that you rounded all the Aborigines up and put them in reserves.

They were trying to deculturise the Murri people. They brought them from all over the state and people were forced to speak English and forget their traditional languages and culture. They were also being very heavily pushed into the whole concept of assimilation and integration, of being more like white Australians. And that meant the government of the day really wanted them to forget their language and their culture and their country.

The extreme end of all of this was that the government believed that Murries would eventually die out and that would solve the whole situation, but of course we all know that didn't happen.

So my parents, who had lived on the Cherbourg reserve on and off for twenty years or so, were pushed into the city. And that's what happened to a lot of Murri people in the late 'forties and early 'fifties. They were being told they had to become more independent of the government, even though the government had created this very dependency through the reserve system.

They moved to Brisbane and I was born there. It was a time when there was a lot of segregation between blacks and whites. Many Murri people at the time had also been indoctrinated to believe that they were inferior to whites and that they had to be more like them if they wanted to be acceptable.

But despite all that, it wasn't that bad, it was good a lot of the time, and my memories of growing up in Brisbane are pretty good. We were always around a lot of Murri people, mostly extended family and people we grew up with. In one form or another there was always some Murri culture happening—the community was always there and it was very strong.

The language situation was that we didn't speak any of our own language. Our parents had been told quite severely that traditional languages were all junk and rubbish—pagan languages even. So it was drummed into our heads that English was the only language that we had to learn, and we were supposed to learn it well.

My strongest memories of Murri languages from when I was growing up are of a very old traditional man who everyone called either Grandfather Willie McKenzie or Uncle Willie McKenzie. It seemed to us children that he had been alive forever, and it was obvious he carried a lot of knowledge about the old days. He was a great storyteller and everyone always wanted to listen to his stories and hear him speak in language. Grandfather Willie spoke many Murri languages from south east Queensland, and even more amazing to a lot of people was the way he spoke perfect English.

Anyway, I have very strong cultural memories of this old man and his language knowledge. We are related to him through our father's father, who was also a traditional man from the Brisbane valley. My father could understand some language, and probably speak it too. But like many Murries of that generation who grew up on reserves, he had been convinced by white government people that these languages were of no use to oncoming generations.

So we weren't taught our language, we were deliberately denied access to this cultural knowledge. Our rights to our language had been deemed by government authorities to be out of our hands, so we were denied access to the languages of our parents and grandparents. It was demanded of us that we learn to speak and write English, so we could be assimilated, integrated, educated, or whatever.

Over the years though I did have limited exposure to other Murri people speaking language. You didn't hear it a lot in a place like Brisbane, but there were words and phrases that people used all the time. Even today there are a lot of words that have survived and Murries still use them. I'm sure all over the country, if you went around different communities you would hear Aboriginal and Islander people using their language, no matter how urbanised they might be.

It wasn't until I got a bit older that I became more interested in language. When I was in my mid-twenties I was travelling by bus across the Nullarbor Plain. In the middle of the night we stopped and this Aboriginal woman and her little girl got off. I was sitting there by the window in the dark, looking out. There was a great big mob of people waiting for her. They were all calling out and speaking in language to her and it was just amazing—I mean I didn't understand a word they said, but they were all very excited about her coming home, her and her little girl. It gave me a real feeling of pride, to hear them all talking, and to know that our languages were still there and being used, and they were very special and very different.

It didn't come to anything until I had the opportunity to go back to school and then on to university when I was in my late twenties. I was friends with another Murri woman, and we both had this really strong idea in our minds that it would be good to understand more about Murri languages.

So we enrolled in some first year linguistic subjects. The

classes were huge, there were hundreds of kids just out of school, and we were mature age students, the only Murris, and thrown into this world of linguistics which was almost like a foreign world. We were also at a bit of a disadvantage because we didn't speak any languages other than English. But I stuck with it, and I certainly was determined once I realised that it was a way of having access to our languages that I would never have the opportunity to do otherwise. So I persevered through University and did a degree in linguistics, and that ended up being something that has changed my whole life, really.

Studying our languages made me realise the tragedy of the situation that we'd been forced into, living in south east Queensland where we've never had access to our languages. I started to understand some of the history behind all that, the history of how our languages were deliberately wiped out. How there was this deliberate cultural and linguistic genocide going on, and that people were made to believe that the only acceptable form of communication and lifestyle was one that mirrored the white one.

As a kid I'd never questioned that, but once I realised these things as an adult there was this real determination in my head that I wanted to be involved with languages, and that language could change things. I think that drove my determination to complete my degree. I felt that I had really been cheated of something—that our identity and our presence in this country had been minimalised and marginalised. And there was always the feeling of, they're trying to kill us off. It becomes very personal.

I was also feeling a lot of resentment, and I had to deal with that as well. It was resentment towards the linguists who were lecturing us about our languages. By this stage my friend had dropped out, and I was the only Murri amongst the undergraduates in the department. And often I'd think, well it's so awful to have to be told about your languages by non-Aboriginal people. Sometimes it made me very angry.

But, on the other hand, one of them was extremely supportive and it was probably due to him that I stuck with linguistics and finished my degree. Once I graduated and started working as a linguist I also realised that a lot of these academics had very good working relationships with the indigenous communities they worked with. It's partly due to their work that some of our languages are now in a position to be maintained and strengthened by the communities.

This is probably a good time to tell you some of the basics about our languages. In Australia two hundred years ago there were at least two hundred and fifty separate language families. Within those language families there were five to six hundred dialects. These days it's estimated that there are still at least a hundred indigenous languages being spoken. I don't think we can take that figure as being an absolute, definite figure.

The numbers of speakers of individual languages vary. Languages like Walpiri and Pitjantjatjara in the centre, and other languages in the Top End might have thousands of speakers—I'd say three to five thousand as a maximum. Then there are languages here in south east Queensland, the areas which were invaded and colonised first, where you might only have a couple of speakers.

They are very complex languages, and often there are different kinds of languages within a language. So you might have an avoidance language which might be a mother-in-law language, or you might have initiation languages. There've been a few theories around as to which languages of the world they might be related to, if they are in fact related to any, but nothing's been established. They're case languages which makes them very different from English, more like Latin for instance.

There are two distinct language groups in Australia. The majority of them fall into a category which is Pama-nyungan languages. And then there's the smaller category, which includes a small group in the Northern Territory and the north of Western Australia, which are non-Pama-nyungan languages.

They are agglutinating languages, which means words are built with bits added on to them, to mark things like case, tense, and aspect. The Pama-nyungan languages generally are suffixing languages, so the extra bits or morphemes are added to the tail of the word. The non-Pama-nyungan languages are generally prefixing languages, which means that the extra morphemes are added to the front of the word. Either way, you can end up with some very long words.

Sign languages are important too, and in some areas they're used a lot and are quite strong and healthy. Sign language was used to communicate across language groups, and also for communicating at a distance. It was used in situations where you weren't allowed to talk, for example if people were in mourning, or if you were out hunting and you had to keep quiet because you were stalking animals. The one I've seen in action was in Central Australia and it's really amazing to watch people using it. They still use it all the time in the Centre, and I'm sure in other parts of the country too. Like the situation with spoken languages, in some places people still use sign language, but only the bits and pieces they remember.

So as I was learning about our languages, I was developing more confidence in myself as an Aboriginal person, and I was becoming much more involved in community things. Up until that time I'd always thought I didn't want to get involved, I would just stay out on the edges and do my own thing and live my own life. But I was more confident in myself once I was at university, and I think that enriched my whole experience as a Murri person. I was able to go out into the community and experience Murri life in a different way to the way I had been living it, and that was a real good thing for me.

By the time I got through my degree I felt a great sense of achievement. I felt I had something to offer the Aboriginal community. But at that stage I still didn't realise I had anything to offer my own people in south east Queensland. I felt I had this qualification as a linguist so I could work with Aboriginal languages, but I would have to go where those languages were spoken—where they're strong. So I had my sights set on going to the Northern Territory.

It was a great experience. I went to Alice Springs, and I started hearing all these different languages. I realised how lucky they were and how unlucky we'd been in terms of history and the survival of language and culture. I don't like to think of our languages in the south east as lost, but we'd certainly grown up thinking access to them was a privilege, not a right. And it was a privilege we'd been denied.

That time in Alice was the time when a lot of those things really sunk in. I didn't become a fluent speaker of any of the languages in Central Australia—I'm not a great language learner. But just working with people in language, and being in a place where our languages are a part of everyday life, I was very proud to be part of that.

It was a very different experience for me, because people who've been fortunate enough to remain on their land usually have been able to be strong enough and isolated enough and together to retain their languages. There's certainly a strong parallel between land and language, and I think that's coming home very strongly to us now in south east Queensland. We've got this battle on at the moment to get recognition of our place here. We're the traditional owners of this land, we do have traditional language, we do have traditional culture. There's been this huge gap over the last fifty to a hundred years where we haven't always practised it, and sometimes it's been forced underground, but it's still our land and we're still here.

A lot of people, even some Aboriginal people, tend to write us off. They think we lost our land to colonisation and the cities, and that's that. We're now making a very strong statement. We're saying no, our culture's not dead, and our languages aren't dead. We've got access to them because we've got records and we've got old people who still remember. If you went to every Murri person in the community I'm sure that you would collect a huge amount of language. To me, language revival work like that is crucial.

It's often very difficult to make people understand what it means for urban Murri people to know that our language has survived and is still accessible to us. Our language is fragmented, and maybe some of it is forgotten, but what's survived is very precious to us, and it's very powerful. To be able to ask what does this mean in our language, or to be able to say to kids in a classroom, here are fifty words you can use—that's really important. It's taken me a long while to understand the strength of it. It's an essential part of our being. It's like our Aboriginality, which is like a religious thing, a spiritual thing. Well, language is part of that.

There was a long time in this country where a lot of Aboriginal people had to live in a vacuum, being made to believe that all they had was a poor copy of white Australian life. Being able to use and hear your own language helps to fill the gap. Being able to turn on the radio and hear songs in Aboriginal language, to see our plays and dances on stage, or in Musgrave Park, it all makes us stronger.

It's true to say that many Aboriginal people today don't feel that language is any longer part of our existence, that it's something of the past and not the present or the future. In some ways that's the hardest thing we're up against in terms of language maintenance and language revival—the whole thing of changing people's attitudes, and convincing them there's a definite purpose to language. I see it as part of our cultural renaissance, part of our efforts to restate our position in this country as the indigenous owners of the land, and to get more respect for our place here.

The processes of language maintenance and revival are difficult, but they're not something that we're going to walk away from. It's a challenge we've accepted. Language is part of us, and it's like our land—it's not something that we easily gave up.

Here in south east Queensland, it's a matter of language revival. In areas like central Australia and the Northern Territory, the challenge is language maintenance. Some linguists, the purists, would probably say that our languages here in south east Queensland are dead. But we don't like to see them that way. I think that if you accept that, then you're accepting that our culture and our language are something of the past, and you give up working to get them back into a healthier state. Those of us Murri people who've been subjected to the extremes of language loss and language deprivation, we believe strongly that it is our birthright to have access to our language and culture.

Language revival is a process of reconstructing a language from fragments. We use a lot of historical data, we put it all together and then we try to match it and bring it to some kind of common core. Sometimes we might know the structure of a related language, and that will help. In the old days when white fellas got interested in the languages and started writing them down, they each did it their own way, so interpreting their material can be tricky. When there's any doubt about pronunciation or usage in the historical record, we take the old people as our guide. If we put their knowledge of the language and pronunciation together with the written records, we can build up a lot of information.

It's interesting to see what words people remember. Mostly they remember body parts and words referring to people. They remember kinship terms, and they remember place names. Often they'll remember sentences, particularly common sentences. Some people remember swear words, not anything like the words people use these days, they're just words you'd use to say something bad about somebody.

But body parts are the main thing—people remember the word *djinang* which is foot, or the word *binang* which is ear. Those are the kind of words which people most commonly remember in south east Queensland. But individuals remember lots of other words too, and I think it would be quite surprising for people if they realised the extent of people's language memories in urban areas.

We also have quite a few people who remember corroboree songs from this area and in the last ten years people have been doing more of the traditional singing and dancing. The versions that you hear now quite often have been modernised a bit, which always happens with language and song. I'm not one of those people who think that the language we speak today has to be exactly the same as the language that the old people spoke fifty years ago. Obviously whatever form of language we start to generate in this community is a form that has been adapted to modern day living and modern day conditions.

The thing that I would like to get over to people is you don't have to be speaking a language daily for it to be important to you. It's just that whole feeling of knowing that your language is there and that you can go and pick up a book and know that this is your language. I'm working on a dictionary, at the moment, of two of the languages of south east Queensland, and I'm hoping that when it's published people will dip into it all the time. I want Murri people from the area to be able to say, oh yeah, we're just going to look up that word in our language.

It's a dictionary for two of the languages from south east Queensland. Technically speaking, they're both the same language, and one is a dialect of the other. They are Gubbi Gubbi, spoken from the Mary River down to the Noosa region, and Butchulla which was the language spoken on Fraser Island where my mother's family comes from.

The information for the dictionary is all there—it's in people's memories, it's in the archives, it's in the libraries, but a lot of it's not really accessible to everyone. I want to make it accessible so they can feel a sense of ownership of the language too. Even though you may not be a fluent speaker, it's still your language, and it's something to be proud of.

Even though I'm working in that technical area now, the

area that's always excited me most as a linguist is the relationship between the social situation and our use of language. I'm particularly interested in the development and changes that happen in language. I'm really interested in the development of pidgins and creoles, and the fact that Murri people might use several different dialects or sociolects of English, and be competent speakers of two or more traditional languages as well.

A pidgin language develops when you've got two completely different cultural and language groups coming together and neither group can speak to each other, so they start speaking a broken down language. It's a mixture of two or more languages, and it just develops because people need some form of communication. It's usually referred to as a contact language.

But when that pidgin is spoken by the next generation of people as their first language, it then has full status as a language, and it's then called a Creole—it develops its own grammar and its own lexicon. Creole is the language that's spoken by the second generation of speakers. And that's what's happened in many parts of Australia, for example in the Torres Strait and in the Northern Territory and Western Australia. The largest number of speakers of any Aboriginal language today is of Creole speakers. It's the fastest growing language in the country as far as Aboriginal and Torres Strait Islander communities go. Many people think that's not a good thing, but I think it's a fact of life.

Still, creoles and Aboriginal dialects of English are an issue in areas where you have strong indigenous languages and you want to maintain them. As with English, pidgins and creoles can have an overwhelming effect on indigenous languages. I believe the only way we can control the effects of Aboriginal English and creole is to encourage communities to use their traditional languages in as many contexts as possible. We need to encourage the younger children in particular, set good role models, and develop language habits which will keep our languages strong.

Even in a community where the languages are strong, language maintenance takes lots of work and resources. The most essential thing, of course, is that you've got to have people willing to do the work. You need language speakers, and people who are willing to go out and record the language. You need to develop books and posters and other teaching materials, and that's a lot of work if you're dealing with a language that doesn't have a written form. So you need human resources and you need money. You need the time and the energy to convince other people around you that this is a good thing and it's a very important thing and it's very worthwhile. That's not always easy because we don't have the funds, and language is not always regarded as a priority.

Most people assume that either the language is there or it's not. But it's not that simple. You have to look at how much exposure people are getting to their language, and the context they're hearing it in. Think about how different it would be if Murri kids were learning their own languages at school, or if they were hearing other Murris speaking language every day. In Brisbane we now have a Murri radio station operating fifteen hours a day, and it makes a real difference. Hearing songs in Aboriginal languages—even though those languages aren't ours, they're not from this area—gives you a feeling of pride.

Just as we can say there's a point in our history when we started to lose some of our languages, we can also point to a time when we saw a resurgence of interest in language. Up until ten or twelve years ago this area had basically been the domain of academic linguists, and some missionary organisations—people who had gone out into the communities with a specific goal in mind. Some wanted a written form of the language so they could do bible translations. Some had a purely academic interest.

Ten, twelve years ago there was a move to get more community involvement in language maintenance and language revival programs. And that was when I got involved.

I'd gone out to Alice Springs to work for Yipirinya School, and I arrived there in 1981. We had a national meeting to set up an Aboriginal Languages Association. People came from all over Australia and the Torres Strait. Eddie Mabo was elected as our first President that year. We took on this whole issue that Aboriginal and Islander people should have more control over what's happening with our languages. So we used to have national meetings once a year, until there wasn't any funding. But it was the beginnings of having a say about what was going on with language.

At the time the federal government was considering a National Language Policy. We got involved and went to meetings in Canberra, there was a lot of discussion at the time. Indigenous people were doing more language work, there were more interpreters being used, there was a greater need for interpreter training, there was a greater need for translation of material. There was also a developing interest in people doing linguistic analysis of their own languages, so there were courses starting up at Batchelor and places like that.

For Murri people this was an area where we could actually be doing something that was really positive, and was adding to the whole business of who we are in this country. People got involved in a practical sense, but also at the policy and funding levels. It was good to be able to know that you had a say in what was going on. When they were talking about our place in relation to English and French and German and Greek and Italian and all the other foreign languages that they had to consider in that context of a National Language Policy, we were there as Murri people, having our say.

For people like me, from a highly urbanised and developed area, it was also important that we were able to say that we had a right to a place in that forum. It's been a bit of a battle to get people to recognise that even though we're from an area where our culture and our language have been pushed underground for the last fifty to a hundred years, we're still Aboriginal people. We might not be language speakers as such, but we regard ourselves as no less Aboriginal than our brothers and sisters in the remote parts of the country. We want other people to see us that way too—to accept our Aboriginality.

The budget for Aboriginal language maintenance and revival isn't very much, three million dollars a year plus a smaller amount under the Aboriginal Education Policy. And it's got to be shared around the whole country. When we come together to look at the budget and the funding issues there are always going to be disagreements in terms of who deserves to have a bigger slice of the cake. But basically the position we take is that those of us who have been more dispossessed by colonisation have as much right as any other groups to be funded for language maintenance and language revival.

Our situation is different to that in the Northern Territory, Western Australia and even North Queensland and South Australia, places where languages are strong. Our job is even harder because we're trying to undo the damage that's been done over the last hundred years and we're trying to change people's attitudes about language. We're trying to get our own mob to be more positive and open to language. We're also dealing with a mass of non-Aboriginal people who don't even realise that indigenous languages have survived. Some are surprised to find that we ever had languages at all!

Sometimes with our own mob, people see money for language programs as a bit of a luxury. They say, well you know, we're talking about survival issues here. We've got people who don't have water, who don't have basic hygiene services; they don't have proper housing. And when you've got a lot of people living way below the poverty line, then it's not surprising some people think we should forget about language until we've got these more immediate things sorted out.

But my argument will always be that if we are stronger in our culture and our language, some of those other things will improve as well. We will be tackling it from a different perspective as stronger people, because we'll be stronger in who we are if we're stronger in our language and our culture. We don't have to copycat the white way of living and we don't have to feel that we're dependent on government handouts. It would add another dimension, and I think it would be a really positive dimension to people's lives. It does give you something.

It's probably hard for non-Aboriginal people to understand how much our own languages enrich our lives as indigenous people. To speak our language, even if we only know a few words, gives us a real connection with our land and our culture. We can never get that from English, no matter how well we speak it. Our languages are much more descriptive of the environment and the landscape they developed in. And they're much more descriptive of relationships in our culture. We have whole kinships systems in Aboriginal society that English just doesn't have accurate terminology for. Some of us have had to relearn that, because we haven't had access to the information and the words for it.

Language also helps us describe our place here more explicitly than we can in English. You've probably noticed around the country that more and more Aboriginal people are going back to the old way of identifying themselves by stating who their tribal group is. So I can say I come from south east Queensland, I'm a Jagera person on my father's side and I'm a Nulingbara person on my mother's side. It's part of the whole protocol of identifying who you are in this land, and for us that is really important. It tells you that we haven't been wiped out. It tells you that we belong to this land, that we have a connection with it that goes right back to the beginning of this country—and in our eyes, life did begin here. It's a statement that we want people to know who we are, and that we do have that knowledge, and that connection to the land that we identify with is as strong as it ever was.

The federal and state governments have acknowledged

that we do have a place in the education system and that our languages do have the right to be maintained and revived. They've given us that recognition in policy documents, they've allocated us funding; it isn't enough but it's there. We're making the most of it, we're trying to get as many programs as possible happening all around the country, we're trying to get more indigenous people involved, and we're trying to get more non-Aboriginal people interested in what's happening with our languages, because we obviously need that support.

We need people to say, yeah, why shouldn't their languages be revived or maintained? It's part of the heritage of this country really—part of the cultural heritage of the country as a whole. To non-indigenous Australians our languages can give a far richer experience of this country. If you're willing to acknowledge our history with the land and our languages, then it has to be a far richer experience than you'd get if you go on denying all of that.

Think of all those Aboriginal and Islander words that are now part of every-day language. They entered the English language because you had no words for those places, concepts, relationships, plants, and animals and the language is richer for it. Aboriginal people do have something special and distinctive to offer this country, and the contribution would be even greater if our own languages were fostered and kept strong.

At a government level, a lot of talk about language is based on economics. There's a real emphasis on trying to get people to learn the languages of our trading partners—so lots of kids are learning Japanese.

I don't think that's a bad thing, I think that anything that can change people's attitudes about language generally is a good thing. But I'd like to see more recognition of the social and spiritual value of language. We're working on that, and we hope that in the next few years there will be curricula developed for our languages to be taught at the secondary level. I think that's the thing that most Aboriginal and

Islander people who have a passionate commitment to language would like to see happen—that our languages would be taught, and given the same respect as foreign languages.

Of course that would involve recognition that they are the indigenous languages of this country, and that the speakers of those languages are still here. It would involve acknowledgement that the languages have gone through excruciating changes, and that we as the people, the speakers of those languages, have had to endure and survive that passage of time as well.

Now, we're making this strong statement. We're saying we haven't lost our languages, we are still here, our languages are still here, our culture's still here, and our land's still here. We want to see our identity as Aboriginal people recognised and respected in all its dimensions. Languages are a very strong part of that, and we want to see respect from non-Aboriginal people in the same way that they regard other languages of the world.

It's a mistake to dismiss our languages as part of history, and long gone. They're not. They are alive and vibrant. They're in a new phase of growth. They're part of us as Murri people, as the indigenous people of the land. Our languages are the voice of the land, and we are the carriers of the languages.

Five

A TORRES STRAIT PERSPECTIVE

Getano Lui (Jnr)

We indigenous peoples live in a truly international world. The United Nations has recognised this fact by making 1993 an international year for all such peoples, including Torres Strait Islanders and Aborigines. As Prime Minister Keating and several prime ministers preceding him have said, Australia is responsible to the world for its policies towards us. However, most Australians continue to think that we are people whose lands, sea, and lives are matters for the convenience of the States and Territories in which we live.

Torres Strait is unique because all of us who live there can never forget for a moment that our world is international and multi-national. We live with the effluents from mines, new development projects and international shipping swirling around in the waters from which we obtain our daily food. When we express concern to government about standards of pollution control, we are told that Indonesia and Papua New Guinea, and world shipping, are immune to Australian interference. This Australian policy may be politically correct, but we Islanders and our children live with its uncertain effects—on our health, the natural resources which are the basis of our livelihoods, and our future.

I must say that in recent years Islanders have been very

frustrated with this state of affairs. Although we believe that the islands, reefs and seas of Torres Strait are ours—a view which has been partially confirmed by the Mabo decision of the High Court—we have almost no power to manage or protect them. Nor do we receive the economic benefit which they provide to others. For these reasons we believe that the growing experience of the international community in recognising indigenous rights is very important. Just as Australians look abroad for new fashions, popular music and medicines, let us look abroad to help improve relations between indigenous peoples and the European society which has established Australia's contemporary governments. (Torres Strait Islanders and Aborigines had their own forms of government and decision-making for thousands of years before Captain Cook, of course.)

Australian governments have sent ministers and officials abroad for many years to gather information on indigenous policy. We do not know if they have learned anything. However, today we indigenous peoples ourselves must help each other and learn from each other.

Let me tell you about a remarkable trip I have just made. The Sami, or Lapp people, of Scandinavia invited me to speak to them about indigenous rights at a special conference they held on the Arctic Ocean coast of Norway. (That ocean is known locally as the Ice Sea, and certainly I have never felt so cold in my life!) Despite the differences in climate, Sami and Torres Strait Islanders are talking about the same problems. We both have high unemployment, but very little control over the fisheries which have sustained our people throughout our history. We both face governments and fishermen from outside our region who deny our rights and who claim that our resources are for them to control. We are both struggling to maintain our languages and cultures. We are both seeking new political structures to enable our people to make decisions for ourselves. One of the people at the conference was the Chief Justice of Norway who wrote a report several years ago insisting that Sami had special rights to the fisheries of their region. That report is having increasing impact on Norwegian government policy.

Several years ago the Norwegian government accepted another report by an indigenous rights commission. That report recommended that the national constitution be amended to recognise that indigenous Sami are a people equal in rights with Norwegians. This was done. The amendment also says that it is the obligation of the Norwegian government to provide Sami the means to maintain and develop their own culture and society. Today the practical implications of this constitutional change are being worked through in different areas of public policy. For instance, there is a need for more and better Sami schools, and many other things.

At the conference in Norway there were also representatives of the Inuit political organisations of Greenland and Canada, and of Indian peoples in North America, and the Maori. They, too, have been making progress in establishing their rights to manage fisheries and marine environments. The United States and Canada both have recent policies as a result of court actions which recognise that indigenous peoples have first rights to fisheries and marine livelihoods. In other words, while here in Australia people are still debating whether Islanders and Aborigines have any rights to a role in coastal and marine areas, the principle is being translated into action overseas. Governments in Australia should note particularly that North American Indians and Canadian Inuit have shown a tougher and more detailed approach to marine conservation and environmental protection thanks to their more intimate and complete knowledge of coastal and marine eco-systems. That is the sort of experience which Torres Strait Islanders can offer Australia in our region.

At the conference several experts from around the world summarised progress on indigenous rights and indigenous self-government. It was clear that Australia has a long way to go to catch up with some other European countries in its treatment of indigenous peoples. However, it was good to see that so many other people were interested in the Australian scene. Many people had visited Australia and everyone had heard of the Mabo decision. It was clear to me that while every indigenous people had some good ideas and some useful experience, every people also had much to learn from the others.

For instance, there was much interest in the Marine Strategy for Torres Straight—what we call MaSTS. We handed out copies of our MaSTS discussion paper which we developed earlier this year with the help of a university scientist. I had a chance to discuss the issues involved with Norway's national Sami leader over lunch one day. The initiative Islanders have shown in that project—encouraging governments and experts to bury their jealousies and work together for the benefit of the marine environment—is one which others may follow.

What government departments with all their experts had been unwilling or unable to do—that is, to focus their experts, funds, and other resources on proper coastal management—we have been able to do. The difference is obviously the commitment of our people to ecologically sustainable development. In other words, environmental protection and sustainable development are not simply matters of formal education and scientific support—they depend in the last analysis on the will of a people to make them work. Islanders have that will, whereas modern industrial Australia has not had it to date. I think there is a very big lesson here.

The day after the conference in Norway a number of university experts took me out to a Sami township in a nearby fjord. The place is called Káfjord and there the former mayor and another local person who had spoken at the conference showed us around. Remember that the days in North Norway were now only a couple of hours of daylight on the southern horizon and that in two weeks the sun would be gone entirely for some months. In this dark and cold world the fjord fishery is the basis of survival for Sami. Development projects of various kinds, and fishing regulations which favour big operators from far to the south, have marginalised the Sami. Now they are developing various ideas for implementing an indigenous fishery. They are also developing other activities such as wool mitten production and the revival of ancient Sami crafts.

What impressed me most, however, was the high quality of housing and public facilities such as roads, schools, and hospitals guaranteed by the Norwegian government. Unlike Australia where areas like Torres Strait are neglected, Norway has laws and policies which make sure that even the most remote communities have high living standards equal to those in the most central places. It is this aspect of life in northern Europe from which Australia may have most to learn.

Of course, some Norwegians think that once Sami have good housing and health care, they should forget about being Sami and just become good Norwegians. Certainly in Australia many people in government think that the indigenous issue is simply one of social programs and job creation. The Sami, however, confirmed what we already knew: that maintaining one's culture, values and traditions is beyond price. Human beings cannot live without that. In Australia it is the Torres Strait Islanders and Aborigines who have a special role in carrying the whole tradition of place. After all, we are at home here, and European people are not. This is reflected in everything from skin cancer statistics to the inability of much Australian industry to operate sustainably in the unique Australian environment. We are glad to share our culture and values with Europeans and other migrants, but we will never give them up. Now the world community has endorsed the importance of our approach in the Rio Earth Summit documents and the Brundtland Report which provided the background to the Earth Summit. It will be interesting to see how long it takes for Australia's official signature on the Rio documents to be translated into daily official actions and regulations in this country.

The reason I mention this Arctic trip of mine is that it shows that even in the place on earth most remote from Australia and most unlike Torres Strait, the problems and needs of indigenous peoples, and the ways in which they relate to governments, are familiar. I was told that it has not been many years since Norwegians and their governments did all they could to suppress Sami language and culture. The change has come with new social attitudes in the general public and more determined indigenous leaders, both of which have emerged since World War II. Just like Torres Strait!

Of course, there are other indigenous peoples who would be glad to have our problems. The conference in Norway heard the Nobel prize-winner, Rigoberta Menchu, speak about genocide in her country, Guatemala. It was once the great Mayan Indian civilisation; today it is a nasty barbaric European dictatorship. We also heard first-hand from a Sami living in Russia about the problems indigenous people face there, daily. She shocked the conference deeply because she told her story so matter-of-factly, and because the problems she discussed are only a few miles from the Norwegian border. She brought home to us all that there is a need to act, and to remember that none of us has far to go to find other people in need.

That is the spirit in which I want Torres Strait Islanders and other Australians to think about this international indigenous year. The year is almost over. The problems of indigenous peoples remain. What have we done about them this year? In Australia we have heard some outrageous statements about the Mabo decision, while we have also seen some principled and firm responses from various politicians, most notably the Prime Minister. I think the lesson we should draw from the international indigenous year is that the time for talk is over. Now we must build a new framework for Torres Strait. We need better services and better decisions. We need more opportunities for our people in school and work. We need the means to develop our Torres Strait way of life.

It is important when we talk about Torres Strait to remember that we are not a simple and isolated people for whom Australia need only provide a few crumbs. We are a distinct people with traditions widely shared in the Pacific region, and we are an indigenous people like nearly three hundred million others around the world. If officials in Brisbane and Canberra like to think of us as people at the end of the line for public services in outback Queensland, we are among those peoples first in line in the world of indigenous people. That is, we are a people living in a First World country—a country which is supposed to be setting the standards in human rights, the exercise of democracy, and socio-economic well-being in the world. Australia has not been doing a very good job in these regards, however, and the world knows it. The question for us now is whether Australians will work with Islanders to improve the situation, or whether the international community of nations, of human rights organisations, and of minority peoples must call on Brisbane and Canberra to do their duty.

Many Australian politicians past and present have used the isolation of this continent to talk and act—especially in matters of race relations—in ways which are unacceptable in other developed countries. We still hear premiers in Australian states telling people that their governments are as progressive and modern as any. This is not true, and it is surprising that the people who know—the media, the academics, business elites, and ordinary people who travel and read with their eyes open—have not corrected the record. Unfortunately we are a nation with many political bullies who think they can shout down the truth.

I think that one great change we will see from now on in Australia is the use of international comparisons and of progress elsewhere to test and improve national policies. It is the Mabo decision more than the Columbus anniversary or the international year which is responsible. That is, by getting rid of the idea of *terra nullius* we have joined the world. The High Court judges specifically referred to legal traditions in other countries in reaching their own decision. Not only judges and administrators are learning new things. Peoples like the Sami and Inuit are learning from the example of the Marine Strategy for Torres Strait, and from other valuable Australian cases. This is very much a two-way process. Now that Australia has joined the world it cannot withdraw again, unless like South Africa in times past it is willing to be despised and boycotted by all decent countries.

Ultimately, of course, Torres Strait Islanders must live daily with their Queensland and Papuan neighbours, and with the politics of our region of the world. This question of the political relations of Torres Strait with Australia and our international region is the central issue we must solve. Everything flows from it. If we have the right political and administrative structures in place we can seek our own solutions to daily problems, be they large or small. We are neglected within Queensland and Australia, but a stronger regional authority will make all the difference.

Let me make one thing clear. Torres Strait Islanders are not trying to abandon Australia. When I hear people accuse us of that I cannot help but think of how in the 1970s the Australian government wanted to give away some of our people and islands to a foreign country. I don't think Australians have anything to teach us about loyalty. But the fact is, today Australia tries to manage our affairs through the representatives of nearly forty official agencies and departments, none of whose officials are accountable to our region or our people. To participate in Australia as citizens we must change this status. I do not wish to prejudge the exact relationship which may develop. Perhaps we will negotiate over the next years some new status—in time for the 2001 anniversary of the Constitution. Whether we and our Australian negotiating partners will find that a specific island territory constitution serves us best, or a new Australian Constitution big enough to embrace Islander and Aboriginal peoples, I cannot tell. We are looking at a range of options. None of those options calls into question our continued association with Australia in culture, spirit or law. We need reforms and improvements, not a separation, and certainly not a divorce.

Australians often forget that there are already three inhabited island territories—Norfolk, Christmas, and Cocos-Keeling—each with its own tailor-made local constitution. Those constitutions are tailor-made to suit local cultural, historical, and environmental realities. There is no reason why a Torrest Strait regional government cannot be devised.

A federation like Australia is made up of different levels. Where and how they fit is a matter for review. The States and Territories today want changes. The Federal government wants changes. Many people across Australia want changes. And the Torres Strait Islanders and Aborigines want changes. We are in a decade of constitutional reform. We can choose to find this threatening, as some reactionaries do, viewing every proposal from any quarter as a threat to national survival. Or, we can be intelligent and optimistic in thinking and talking about improvements needed to benefit our people and all people in this country. As a board member of the Constitutional Centenary Foundation, I am an optimist. I also know that constitutional reform is not some radical agenda but a process begun by the leading politicians in Australia and being carried forward by some of the most distinguished experts and public figures in Australia. This is the real world in which Torres Strait is seeking to improve its political relationships, not some fantasy scenario of separation imagined by a hysterical policy think-tank. (One of the Canadian Inuit leaders calls them sink-tanks, and often they are!)

The principles for Torres Strait constitutional renewal are simple. We need to be able to make decisions about social, cultural, economic, and environmental matters in our region, not just the right to attend advisory meetings which may, or may not, pass our ideas up the line. We need a clear, legally enforceable regime of land and sea rights. We need real control of staff and office budgets, not the appearance of control as through ATSIC. We need the means and facilities to secure and develop our culture. We support the right of mainland-dwelling Islanders to services and institutions which are culturally appropriate where their numbers locally warrant it. There are many ways in which such needs may be packaged. We are prepared to sit down and work out the details with government.

We should be aware that by world standards this is a moderate program for change. Of course, our aim is not to seem moderate or radical, but to meet the needs of our people. Successful political reform in Torres Strait will depend on matching local needs and experience to proven precedents and workable, straightforward structures. In these matters we must always rely on the will and ingenuity of our people in making any arrangements work. Islanders have acquired useful experience through the local government community councils and the Island Co-ordinating Council. Now it is time to move on.

Torres Strait Islanders do not participate in Australia today on anything like the same footing as most non-Islanders. When we are able to do so on the basis of the sort of principles I have outlined, most of the grievances of our people will be gone. That is when we can talk about Australian 'reconciliation' and Australian 'unity'.

What sort of world lies ahead for Torres Strait? The world-wide commitment to ESD—to ecologically sustainable development—offers particular hope to regions like ours. It is built on small-scale, renewable resource values, and on the traditional knowledge of local people. That is precisely the sort of society which flourished in Torres Strait for thousands of years. We need a mix of enterprises and skills. We need to combine imported technology and local experience. We need the commitment and understanding of local authorities accountable to Islanders.

We are fortunate to have already living in Torres Strait a

mixed population who are truly at home, from many parts of the South Pacific, Asia, and Europe. Thursday Island is the most multi-racial community in the Australian world. These people bring many skills to add to those traditional to the Torres Strait Islander community. Our destinies are all linked together in our region. The well-being of Islanders can only increase the well-being of others living there. Just as land claims and self-government settlements in other countries have generated a regional mini-boom, we may expect the same sort of effect in Torres Strait. Our concept of the future is one in which resident non-Islanders are every bit as much a part as those whose roots are in our Islands.

The range of economic options for Torres Strait may be very limited. After all, since the decline of pearling the world of conventional development has largely passed by our region. That means that entrepreneurs have not been attracted by local opportunities. It is easy to see that fisheries development of many kinds is the major regional hope. The need for an effective administrative presence in the region to cope with growing border problems, and the requirements for public services for local people indicate growth for the public sector. We want to see Islanders benefitting from that growth and being trained for those positions. There is also a need for a wide range of niche markets and small enterprises. Our people had to use a range of skills and engage in many different activities in the past and we can do so again.

A difficult problem for today's governments in Australia is their top-down mentality. The various international commitments Australia has made in respect of indigenous peoples require that local cultures and peoples are supported. That is, local differences are important, and must be recognised in policy. While governments are concerned about streamlining their delivery of public services, they are starting at the wrong end of the problem. Our need, as confirmed by international conventions, is for the strengthening of local and regional identity. Torres Strait is not an interim society or passing culture. We are a people who intend to survive with a distinct culture and society. The international agreements which Australia has signed entitle us to government policies which help us. In Norway, I learned, Article 27 of the United Nations' Civil and Political Rights convention of 1966 has been interpreted to include protection of the natural resources and their use by indigenous peoples. This interpretation is now spreading and is becoming the international standard. We will be reminding the Australian authorities of this when we discuss fisheries and marine resources.

Islanders do not have stars in their eyes. We know that political reform will take hard work. We know that to become a healthy regional community our own initiative and the commitment of our people are needed. That being said, we need support and resources. In other countries the governments have come to realise that spending on indigenous peoples is not a financial loss. If more people are able to participate positively in the society and economy of the country, there is a net gain. There are also smaller social costs for maintaining individuals in hospitals or jails.

Torres Strait is a small region with great resources in the sea. We are a people without as much bitterness as some mainland peoples who have suffered more direct dispossession. It would be easy for Australia to work with us to make our region a success story and a proof to the Asia-Pacific region, and to European sceptics, that modern Australia has turned its back on the racist policies of the past. We are not interested in listing grievances and dwelling on past mistakes. We are looking ahead. But we want a partnership; we do not want an army of social workers to arrive and try to create some bureaucratic paradise in our islands. It is interesting that when one looks at other indigenous situations, those paternalistic approaches—well documented by Jeremy Beckett in his classic anthropological study of Torres Strait—have been just as powerful as resource management problems in fuelling indigenous political movements. What we want now is recognition as a unique cultural and political community in the Australian federation system. For our part, we believe we can contribute a great deal to Australia.

Studies overseas have found that indigenous peoples often go through a phase which outsiders call 'apathy' when their culture and society have been overwhelmed by outside forces. In such situations governments often make paternalistic laws and apply degrading systems which stifle people and prevent their recovery later. That has happened in Torres Strait. We are prepared to take responsibility for ourselves to a much greater degree than we have been allowed. I am talking about real needs. We want to solve our local health problems, get our people working, make sure our young get good schooling, and ensure that our local resources are well managed so that they will provide a living for many generations to come. We are not trying to build our own navy or develop unnecessary institutions. Our aims are practical.

The future is full of uncertainties, and all the people at the conference in Norway were deeply affected by the horrors in the former Yugoslavia. We live in a dangerous world. When the Nobel Institute held a special conference on the world situation in Norway in August 1993, none of the papers given by experts from around the world foresaw a quiet or harmonious time ahead. Issues like mass migrations of people from dictatorships—or to economic opportunities—will require firm action. Environmental crises will require emergency responses. Global disruptions in oil supply or any number of other items may force governments to dictate rationing and other measures which seem tough. The world may be smaller and more inter-related today than in the past, but it is also fragile. Australian governments will soon be forced to take drastic action in various policy areas, and they will be widely supported when they do so. The notion that we live in an era when governments can abandon their roles is nonsense. The need for leadership has never been greater. The reason why some action will be needed—for instance, in environmental areas—is precisely because governments have failed to act earlier.

In other words, our governments will have to rely on the unity and shared ideals of Australia's national role in society more than ever. They must act not only to respond to international crises, but to domestic crises. These include indigenous deaths in custody, unacceptable social disparities, and the grievances which make for racial division. In Torres Strait we already have a crisis. Drugs, arms, illegal migrants, feral species, and disease are threatening Australia, but they are threatening Torres Strait Islanders first. We have offered our experience and our commitment to the Australian authorities in dealing with these matters. As happened in World War II, we find ourselves once again on the front lines of Australian history. Perhaps this time Australians are ready to accept us as equals in the reformed constitutional and social community we hope for in the year 2001.

Six

INTERNATIONAL EFFORTS

Helen Corbett

As a young Yamagee-Noongar woman, it was never my dream to wander outside of my home territory in the state of Western Australia. I never thought I'd travel across the Nullarbor Plain to the eastern seaboard, let alone outside Australia. But somehow I've come to spend much of the last eighteen years lobbying internationally for Aboriginal rights.

Many people, including many indigenous Australians, assume that Aboriginal and Islander issues are purely domestic matters. But we have much to gain from the international arena. We can learn from other countries' attempts to achieve justice for indigenous people. And for Aboriginal and Islander people, there's the chance to use the broad principles on human rights established in the international community. We can use those to encourage the Australian government into action.

I'm often asked where I first started. I would have to answer that I was very much influenced by the events of the civil rights and anti-war movements in America, as well as the anti-apartheid movement around the globe, and especially in Australia. It was the Perth-based Campaign Against Racial Exploitation, or CARE, and their campaign against apartheid in South Africa that got me started in international work. It was a time when shoppers were being encouraged not to buy South African frozen fish, as part of an overall global economic boycott campaign.

From the mid 1970s I regularly attended the annual meeting of the Federal Council for the Advancement of Aboriginals and Torres Strait Islanders. It was a forum that provided a chance for both young and older indigenous Australians to come together from around the country. Many of the well known activists you hear today had their political training in that forum.

In 1972 a group of Aboriginal delegates attended a black festival in Nigeria, and they came home with a new perspective. They were very much influenced by the liberation movements in Africa, where people were going through a decolonising process. I shared a student house with one of them and came into contact with the others. I was also married to a man who left Malaysia because of the problems associated with the decolonising process there. So there was a lot of talking about these ideas.

I remember at one of the last Federal Council conferences, they successfully voted for a name change, to become the National Aboriginal and Islander Liberation Movement. However, not all Aboriginals shared this vision and soon after this body collapsed. Australian media at that time were covering the armed struggled on the African continent, and there was a gross misunderstanding that these Aboriginal people were advocating violence and armed struggle.

Our international lobbying efforts have not always been straightforward. Aboriginal delegations asked African members of the Commonwealth to boycott the 1982 Brisbane Games. It was to be a protest over the federal and state governments' abrogation of their international responsibilities to protect Aboriginal peoples' human rights. They were knocked back, and the African nations attended the games. This rejection gave Aboriginal peoples a new perspective on where to seek international support. It was obvious it wasn't enough to expect help from nations just because they were black. We had to lobby the major international organisations.

My family moved to Sydney in the late 1970s. My career there as Director of Studies at Tranby College and a teacher of political economy helped to speed up my international work. Tranby College is a community-based educational centre whose students and staff come from all around Australia. It's famous as a port of call for indigenous peoples and dignitaries from all around the world. Many of them were guest lecturers in our classes. We went so far as to provide Spanish lessons for those Aboriginals who wanted to use the language to have dialogue with indigenous Spanish speakers from South and Central America. We organised for Tranby students to go on study tours overseas, including Indonesia, Canada and Nicaragua.

In my twenty-three years of working for Aboriginal community-based organisations, Tranby was the only one that continuously and actively promoted the international links between indigenous peoples. It was in this environment that I decided to go on my first international trip and be a part of an Australian/New Zealand work brigade to Cuba and Nicaragua. I was particularly impressed by how they were dealing with racism, and by their policy of involving women in all arenas of social, economic and political life. And their literacy campaign was inspiring. Here was an attempt to bring all members of their society to a certain place of 'knowing', so they could all actively participate.

In 1984 I co-founded the National Committee to Defend Black Rights with the aim of stopping Aboriginal deaths in custody. It eventually became an international campaign, but that wasn't a calculated decision. It was more a matter of being in the right place at the right time.

Aboriginal people have always had an interest in nuclear disarmament because of the effects of nuclear weapons tests in our country. So it was through that connection that I attended the fourth European Nuclear Disarmament Conference in Coventry, England in 1987. We were then given financial support from the London-based Anti Slavery Society, which is the oldest human rights organisation in the world, and incorporates the Aboriginal Protection Society. They funded me to attend the United Nations Working Group of Indigenous Peoples and I have continued with this task up to this year.

I was fortunate that on that first trip there were a lot of people to help me and give advice as to what to do. They were shocked to hear our statements on the deaths in custody issue, and many of them still keep a close liaison with us on this. Each year we give an update on the issue, as well as on other concerns.

The Australian government has been highly embarrassed by international discussion of Aboriginal deaths in custody. In fact it announced a Royal Commission into deaths in custody just a short time after our maiden speech at the UN Working Group. They have spent many hours trying to convince this UN forum, and prominent international human rights organisations, that they are dealing with the issue in the right manner.

However the international community has thought otherwise. During our international campaign the governments of South Africa, France, the United States, and the former Soviet Union have all condemned Australia for its lack of action. Why these particular countries? Simple: Australia had condemned them for their human rights records, and they responded by speaking out on Australia's hypocrisy. They've condemned Australia's failure to address the issue of people dying in Australian police and prison cells, and all the circumstances that put us there in the first place.

People have often asked me what it was like to make a maiden UN speech. I have had a mixed reaction. At first, I considered this forum to be just another chance to speak the truth, and the fact that it was the United Nations had no significance for me. But I was also very nervous. On the actual day, the other Aboriginal delegates and I came early to the meeting to have breakfast at the UN cafeteria. As I had already had mine, I decided to sit in the meeting and read through my speech. For some reason, the speaking order was changed, with the result that I was the only Aboriginal delegate in the room when we were called on to speak. I hit the panic button, and thought maybe I should pretend I wasn't there, but then I thought that would be irresponsible. So I raised my hand, my microphone was turned on, and I began. It wasn't until after that I realised I still had my sun-glasses on!

During my presentation, one of the Aboriginal delegates came back into the room and sat down next to me. She realised that she had missed her turn to speak, so she decided to go outside for a coffee. I can remember presenting my speech, while trying to manoeuvre my leg to trap her in her chair, to make her stay with me because I was so nervous.

As I became more experienced with UN procedures, I formulated a co-ordinated working strategy with the other Aboriginal delegates when we presented our country report in 1990. Previously, indigenous delegates had been allowed ten minutes each, but the Aboriginal delegates might be speaking for ten minutes here and there over the fortnight. I organised for us all to speak one after the other, and to co-ordinate our presentation as a country bloc. Each delegation is able to maintain its own independence within this common strategy. Delegates from the government-initiated Aboriginal and Torres Strait Islander Commission and the Human Rights and Equal Opportunity Commission have recognised the value in this strategy and joined the Aboriginal non-governmental lobby group on this platform.

Other indigenous peoples and also government representatives at the Working Group have commented that the Aboriginal and Torres Strait Islander delegations' strategy has been valuable to them, because it's the only time that they can get a comprehensive and extensive view about a particular government and its relationship with indigenous people. It is interesting to note that the Australian government's contributions to this forum are getting longer and longer. They're dealing with wider issues, trying to cover anything they think the Aboriginal delegations will raise.

International lobbying is often misunderstood. Many people assume it's glamorous and extravagantly funded. But that's not the case. Indigenous delegates often travel on a shoe-string. It's also physically and mentally exhausting. For instance, in 1989 I took with me 1000 booklets on our campaign against deaths in custody. Each day I carried a shopping bag full of the booklets and put them on the information desk at every working group meeting. I did the same with all the Geneva-based international human rights organisations.

It was very difficult to get some Australian funding bodies to see the importance of the international work. In fact some of them surprised me with their sheer ignorance and paternalistic views of the connection between domestic and international lobbying. The character assassination of those Aboriginal people working internationally also disturbed me, coming from so-called progressive Australian social justice organisations. The situation in Australia has changed little today.

It is my personal opinion that the issue of Aboriginal deaths in custody, as one issue, can clearly demonstrate the effectiveness of international lobbying. Each successive year since 1987, the federal government has been forced to account to the UN forums for how it is dealing with this issue. It has forced them to address it. But we still haven't seen satisfactory results, and so we need to keep up this international pressure. Especially given that, two years after the Royal Commission has ended, we're seeing an increase in rates of incarceration and death.

Keeping the international pressure on UN members is a task shared by all indigenous peoples around the globe. Indigenous people first began using the United Nations as a forum back in the 1920s, when American Indians approached the then League of Nations. This was followed by sporadic appeals to world organisations until in 1926 the

International Labour Organisation launched studies of indigenous workers. In 1948 the Bolivian Government appealed to the UN to create a special sub-commission to study the social problems of aboriginal populations. And in the early 1950s the ILO launched a multi-disciplinary development program for indigenous inhabitants of the Andes region in America.

This was followed in 1957 by the adoption of ILO Convention 107 on Indigenous and Tribal Population—the first international instrument dealing with indigenous peoples. It was a document that made it a duty of governments to integrate indigenous people within their country. Its assimilationist approach was rejected by indigenous peoples around the world. In 1989 this convention was reformed, and the Federal Government is now asking Aboriginal people whether it should ratify this new convention, to make it binding on Australia in international law.

Within the United Nations itself, things began to change in 1970 when the Sub-commission on Prevention of Discrimination and Protection of Minorities recommended the establishment of the R. Martinez Cobo report. This report focused on national and international measures to eliminate discrimination. In anticipation of the report's recommendations, the UN Economic and Social Council created the Working Group of Indigenous Peoples in 1982. Since then, this forum has become the biggest UN forum dealing with human rights. Its two agenda items include the promotion and protection of human rights and fundamental freedoms of indigenous peoples, with special attention to the development of standards concerning the rights of indigenous peoples.

After eight years the Working Group produced a Draft Declaration on the Rights of Indigenous Peoples. The draft was finalised this year. The concern of all indigenous peoples now is how to protect some of the rights within the draft document as it moves up the hierarchy of the UN system. There are some hostile governments in the hierarchy, so we're a long way from a final ratified document.

In 1990 the UN adopted a resolution proclaiming 1993 as the World Year of Indigenous Peoples, with the theme of 'Indigenous People: a New Partnership'. The idea was to address human rights, environment, development, education and health issues of concern to indigenous peoples. Generally speaking, there has been a feeling that the year has not achieved its aims. At the World Conference on Human Rights in Vienna in June this year there was a resolution to establish a Decade for the World's Indigenous Peoples, to start in 1994. It is interesting to note here that the Australian government strongly supported this idea of a decade, even though they had decided not to inject additional funds into the international year at a domestic level. Instead, they had instructed government agencies to use their existing budgets to promote the year.

Aboriginal people in Australia began lobbying within the UN system in 1980 when the National Aboriginal Conference representatives attended the Sub-commission on Prevention of Discrimination and Protection of Minorities. They wanted to highlight their concerns about the Noonkenbah situation in Western Australia, where the Aboriginal community was facing the destruction of its sacred sites by an oil exploration company, and a plenitude of diamond exploration leases. The World Council of Indigenous Peoples gave up their allocated speaking time to allow Aboriginal delegates to present this issue.

In 1981, the National Federation of Aboriginal Land Councils attended the same meeting. With the establishment of the UN Working Group in 1982, other Aboriginal organisations attended, including the National Aboriginal Legal Services Secretariat, the National Committee to Defend Black Rights, the National Coalition of Aboriginal Organisations, the Northern, Central, Kimberley and New South Wales Aboriginal Land Councils, and the Top End Coalition. In recent years a conscious effort has been made to increase the number of Aboriginal women and youth delegates.

The increased pressure on the United Nations to open its doors to the non-governmental sector—the NGOs—has meant that indigenous peoples have been able to enter the UN in forums outside the Working Group. These include the UN Conference on the Environment and Development, the UN World Conference on Human Rights, and other special UN technical meetings and forums. Aboriginal people have been involved in these forums. This year for the first time, an Aboriginal NGOs' adviser was appointed (by Aboriginal organisations) to take up the Australian Government's offer for an indigenous adviser on its delegation at the World Conference on Human Rights in Vienna, Austria.

The number of Aboriginal organisations and individuals working in the international arena is still small, but steadily growing. The National Committee to Defend Black Rights is one example where an organisation's membership is trained in this area. Its members have been sent to international forums and speaking tours in West Germany, Switzerland, The Netherlands, Estonia, England, Belgium, Norway, Brazil, and Canada, as well as to the UN forums. It has been mainly Aboriginal women and youths who have represented them.

I want to look now at the Australian Government's record in the international arena. The 1993 Oxford University Press report on the UN members' human rights records listed the Australian record as worse than many other developed Western nations, and some recently emerged Eastern bloc countries. This was because of its poor treatment of indigenous peoples and women. This study is recognised by the UN as an instrument for measuring countries' adherence to international human rights standards.

In 1967 a national referendum gave the federal government the power to legislate on Aboriginal affairs, but successive governments have been reluctant to use these powers, especially when it involves conflict with the states. As a signatory to various international agreements and treaties, the federal government also has the power to intervene in state issues.

Ironically, the battle over the Franklin River—an environmental debate—is the best known case in which a federal government used its external powers to protect an Aboriginal site against state government plans. In a desperate bid to win the environmental vote, the Labor Party had promised to stop the dam. When it came to the court battle with the Tasmanian Government, the Federal Labor Government called on its international obligations to protect world heritage. And one of the factors that gave the area world heritage status was the presence of two caves, once occupied by Aboriginal people. These are the southernmost point on the globe where a record of human occupation has been found, and they would have been flooded by the dam.

Of course the Federal Government's main concern was to keep environmentalists on side. The Tasmanian Government was more straightforward—simply put, they argued that no Aboriginals lived in that state, even though they were receiving federal funding for this community! It is interesting to note here that in the published federal-state response to the 339 recommendations from the Royal Commission into Aboriginal Deaths in Custody, the Tasmanian Government's response is absent! One can only wonder if they really believe the racist doctrine that the last Tasmanian was Truganini.

In the ninety-two years since federation, no federal government has introduced national land rights legislation. With that track record, it's no wonder that Western Australian Premier Richard Court feels confident in proposing a challenge to the Federal Government's Mabo bill. The Western Australian Government basically argues that Aboriginal peoples in this State can't have any property rights. This, and the Federal Opposition's proposal that native title be left to the States to decide, are based on sheer arrogance and racism. Of course they want it left to the States to decide—because it's not the States, but the Federal Government which is the United Nations member and must answer for its record on human rights.

The hysteria and lack of leadership surrounding the Mabo decision further demonstrate the political immaturity of Australia in the international arena. The nature of the dialogue has been set by both the Federal Government and mining and pastoral interests. Aboriginal people have not been major participants in this debate. The debate has been further reduced to a legal question of land management issues, with little to no reference to the human rights of Aboriginal people.

While it had to be the High Court that reversed *terra nullius* and recognised native title, the legal arena and its language are far too narrow to negotiate Aboriginal rights in their entirety. You have to remember that our whole culture is connected to land. So we need to look beyond narrow legal arguments and turn to those broader principles of human rights as they're spelt out internationally. The whole legal arena is currently under review for gender bias. If it can't accommodate white western women, who are half the population of its own culture, how can it accommodate our culture?

Aboriginal views on the Mabo decision are as wide as this country itself, but the Federal Government's framework for consultation is limiting. It's a widely accepted international principle that indigenous people have the right to choose their own institutions and their representatives. This is not a simple thing to achieve. The successive government policies over 200 years, coupled with their continual co-option of Aboriginal activists, has contributed to a lack of Aboriginal leadership.

Australia is not alone with this task of working out arrangements with indigenous peoples within its borders. There are many other examples around the globe where governments have been able to sit down with indigenous peoples and work out arrangements with them. Australia needs to seriously enter the international debate on indigenous peoples so a better and constructive dialogue and arrangements can take place in this country. Australia can learn from other nations, such as the Nordic, Danish, Canadian and Brazilian governments.

For example, it was many years ago, in 1905, that the migratory rights and pasturage privileges of the Sami peoples were respected in the desert lands between Norway and Sweden, at the time that the two countries dissolved their union. The Sami confirmed this arrangement with Finland in 1917. The Greenland Home Rule government in Denmark, and the demarcation of Yanomoni territory in the Amazon basin by the Brazilian government are some further examples where governments have had to work out relationships with indigenous peoples within their borders.

Recently I visited Belgium and spoke to the European Economic Community, its Commission and Parliament, to establish links with them on issues of concern to Aboriginal people in Australia. Currently there are debates to establish permanent forums for indigenous peoples within this structure, as well as developing codes of conduct for business investors. This has included a resolution to ensure that if funds from its Inter-Development Bank go to countries which have indigenous peoples, the countries receiving the monies must consult with the indigenous peoples affected by the development projects.

The World Bank is also currently rewriting its funding guidelines to require indigenous consultation. An example is that the governments of Paraguay, Argentina and Brazil must involve the Guarani people on the Parana River before they can get further funding for the hydroelectric scheme there. It's interesting to note that in this international context, Australia supported the principle of indigenous consultation.

There is a wealth of international indigenous-government experience for Australia to learn from if it wants to be considered as a serious player in this arena. If not, it will continue to be seen for what it is, and that is as an international delinquent.

International and domestic indigenous lobbying are not mutually exclusive, as the above examples demonstrate. Indigenous peoples throughout the world are becoming increasingly aware of this. They have been networking internationally for many years, both amongst themselves, and with non-indigenous organisations. Aboriginals have been a part of this, with their membership of international bodies. The World Council of Indigenous Peoples third General Assembly in 1981 in Canberra was hosted by Aboriginals. Just this year, we have hosted three international indigenous conferences, as well as attending those in other countries. It has to be recognised that domestic legislation and actions help provide a forum for international law to be formulated. In turn, those international legal standards have a binding effect on the behaviour of governments.

International standards are our safety net. And in the international arena we can be certain we'll get our own government's attention. It's a pity we have to go so far from home to do that, but it's proved effective. This is the front edge of the dialogue on human rights, and Aboriginal voices have to be a part of that.

Seven

MABO: Towards respecting equality and difference

Noel Pearson

The Boyer Lectures of the eminent Australian anthropologist Professor William Stanner entitled *After The Dreaming* hold their own amongst this country's finest writings on matters black and white.

Today, more than ever, the series which Professor Stanner delivered for the ABC in 1968 makes compelling reading. His lectures articulate, illuminate and provide some guidance, with questions that will consume the people of this continent for as long as we need to consider them. Such questions as: the future of nationhood and the equivocal citizenship of those with whom a settlement of great grievance remains outstanding; indigenous rights and notions of new partnerships; constitutional and institutional renovation; the never-decreasing need for social reconstruction and renewal; and the great imperative for an equitable distribution of the hitherto not so common weal.

Stanner wrote one year after the 1967 Referendum which, amongst other things, finally incorporated into the Commonwealth the indigenous people of the country. In this lecture I propose to reflect on some aspects of Stanner's lectures, whilst tracing some of the developments of the past two decades, leading to the watershed decision of the

High Court of Australia on 3 June 1993 on the question of native title to the Murray Islands in the case brought by the late Eddie Mabo and others.

I stood but a child of tender years when Professor Stanner spoke hopefully about our entry with a vengeance into the country's history. To tell the story of that time and the changes which have happened and the changes which, like Stanner, we still await, it is appropriate first to tell of the man who commandeered Aboriginal policy in the State of Queensland for more than two decades.

In 1989, on a bright Sunday morning, Joh Bjelke-Petersen stood at the front of the old church at Hope Vale, surveying the long wide street, framed by mango trees and frangipannis with barking dogs idly chasing horses.

Earlier the former State Premier, whose once authoritarian aspect had by now waned considerably, had regaled the congregation of black faces in the weather-board church with stories. Stories of how they had transformed dense woodland into paddocks and rows of tin shacks with wide streets, named after German missionaries now long departed. How they had built this glorious church from the timber that had stood on the paddocks where cattle now grazed. He had returned to the mission to commemorate a community milestone: it was forty years since the Guugu Yimithirr people had returned, largely through his agency as a young Country Party backbencher, from seven years' exile in central Queensland. The mission which had been established in 1886 was closed down in the war, and the people removed when the resident German missionary was interned in 1942.

After the church service, a journalist asked the former Premier about land tenure for the people of the community. With perhaps accidental candour he replied that the land had always belonged to the Guugu Yimithirr. It was just that the Government had been looking after it for them. And now they had handed the land back to the rightful owners.

It was a startling admission—*that the land had always*

belonged to them—from one who had made an international reputation of denying Aboriginal human rights in the State of Queensland and had steadfastly opposed the notion that indigenous people had certain inherent, traditional rights to their homelands. His Government could scarcely bring itself to mention the word 'traditional' without suffering acute political nausea.

In the early years of government policy, Aborigines were different and, because of their alleged backwardness, could be treated unequally. Discriminatory treatment of the mission and reserve inmates during those years, when it was said *we lived under the Act*, arose out of their constitutional perceived lack of quality: black people were innately unequal, therefore special laws where the State governed aspects of peoples' lives which were beyond the reach of law makers for other citizens were justified.

This policy of innate difference and inequality was underpinned by a policy of assimilation for, by a process of training, civilising and indeed *breeding out* their backwardness, the blacks could lose their difference and become like everyone else. They could come out into the mainstream society as people exempted from the Act and finally equal. The Churches would assist in this endeavour and to that end no church body broke more sweat than the Hope Vale Lutheran Mission Board under Bjelke-Petersen's ten-year chairmanship.

My parents watched their contemporaries pack up their young families, leave the mission and go south to live near Lutheran congregations: to milk cows, pick peanuts, cut cane and work on highways. Just like poor whites did.

I don't recall wishing that my family had also gone south. But I do recall the strange tolerance that my father and the older people showed those who administered the paternalistic regime which was our life in the mission: the missionaries and the managers. This was explicable by their over-riding devotion to the Church, a fierce sense of the mission's history and the community's tribulations and survival through times of extreme hardship, loss and dislocation. Like those born before us and indeed those who would follow, the collective psyche of myself and my schoolmates was dominated by the Moses-like figure of George Heinrich Schwarz of Neuendettelsau, who had died six years before I was born.

Old missionary Schwarz had first landed at Cape Bedford in 1887, by which time Guugu Yimithirr people had been reduced to a demoralised fringe-dwelling existence following the establishment of Cooktown. Many of their number now exterminated, their bones lined the blood-stained tracks to the Palmer River Goldfields. There was gratitude for Schwarz's lifelong effort to provide a shelter from a colonial storm whose waves had almost completely swamped the Guugu Yimithirr, drowning many of the descendants of those who first met James Cook at the Endeavour River in 1770.

Who of those who saw the sails disappear north after the crew of the *Endeavour* had effected repairs on the vessel, would have thought that four generations later the Captain's descendants would return with such vengeance, with a fever for gold and for land, leaving demoralised strugglers, begging, sneaking and apologising for an existence in their own country?

Given the Church's role in the secular administration of the mission, and the fact that the Government was now headed by a *church friend*, indeed a *mission friend* during the years of my early youth, the older people forgave and suffered government paternalism in much the same way that they had suffered the paternalism of old Missionary Schwarz.

But as with the old missionaries who had gone, there was increasing disquiet among the younger people about the Government and Church-sanctioned policy of inequality justified by difference. Why were people prohibited from buying motor-vehicles, why should they have to seek permission from the Manager to leave the Reserve, why did the money that they earn have to be kept and managed by the Mission, why could not the community have title to their land in their own hands?

The increasing awareness that Queensland legislation and policies concerning Aboriginal people breached fundamental human rights, and that our *mission friend* was a leading and vehement opponent of Aboriginal rights, brought on a significant identity crisis for the community. It was a crisis which led to a realisation that paternalism whilst in a fraternal context might be a natural relationship of affection, but when it concerned adults of different races it was undeniably racist, and arose from a fundamental assumption of inferiority and superiority. The Government and indeed the Church had assumed our innate inferiority and their own superiority. Like many paternal relationships put asunder, the bitterness of this realisation was painful.

As with the memory of the old Missionary, the pain was most acutely felt by those who had watched their parents and grandparents endure a system which treated them as State wards, as incapable and undeserving of equality and dignity. It was within the young hearts of those who contemplated this history that indignation burned, and it found resonance in the memories and secret, long-suppressed feelings of those who had endured it.

There arose a movement for change and a demand for equality.

The Brisbane Commonwealth Games in 1982 and Aboriginal protests focused international attention on Queensland's record on human rights and land rights in particular, and signalled a change in the direction of the National Party Government's policies on Aboriginal Affairs. The infamous *Aborigines Act* was repealed and new and less draconian legislation governing communities was introduced. Together with legislation granting a form of land title to Aboriginal Reserves under an instrument called a Deed of Grant in Trust, this heralded a new era where the Government strove to address the long-standing and widespread criticisms of its discriminatory laws.

Rather than sanctioning difference and inequality, the new policy urged equality and sameness. Aboriginal people were no longer to be distinct from the rest of the Queensland community, they were equal and this meant that they could not be allowed to be different. Aborigines were to be considered merely dark-skinned Queenslanders.

Communities which had endured terrible histories of repression and stranglehold government management, in which social problems were rife, lacking basic health, housing, educational and other services, were by semantic fiat to have been transformed into wholesome country towns with black yokels sitting on verandahs contemplating cows and the sorghum harvests.

Formal equality was now largely a fact. The Government's policies were therefore difficult to reproach. The response was always that it now treated Aborigines as equal *like any other Queenslanders.*

Of course, the respect in which Aborigines were most similar to their fellow Queenslanders was that they had no special claim or right to their traditional homelands. Non-Aboriginal Queenslanders had no such inherent rights, and it would be discriminatory to accord *special rights* to compensation or land ownership to Aborigines. All rights to land in the State were granted by the Crown and there was neither any legal nor moral claim on behalf of indigenous people to what they claimed were their lands. How can you have an equal society when one group sets itself apart with claims to separate rights?

Therefore, whilst a substantial change occurred in policies in the 1980s from inequality and difference to equality and sameness, both policies were discriminatory and were premised on a vehement denial of the notion of traditional rights to land.

Thus whilst Professor Stanner confronted the myth of waste and desert lands and said that if Crown title were paraded by, every Aboriginal child would say, like the child in the fairy tale, 'But the Emperor is naked ...', in Queensland the Government continued to insist that the Emperor was decently attired in its Crown titles. It was on this insistence that the Bjelke-Petersen Government moved at a night sitting of the Parliament to pass the *Queensland Coast Islands Declaratory Act 1985*. This Act purported to retrospectively extinguish any native title that might have existed in the Murray Islands. If valid, the legislation would bring to an end the court action brought by Eddie Mabo and others three years before, challenging the Crown's power to grant title to people who claimed they already held a pre-existing title to their homelands.

Before dealing further with the question of pre-existing title and the outcome in what is the most important and controversial decision of the High Court of Australia, I would like to survey briefly the developments which unfolded at the national level following the 1967 Referendum and Stanner's hopes for a final breaking of the Great Australian Silence and his hopes for Aboriginal land rights recognition.

Prior to his Boyer lecture, Professor Stanner had been to Yirrkala on the Gove Peninsula, consulting the Aboriginal people in relation to bauxite mining leases granted to Nabalco. He spoke in his lecture about the people's anxiety about the proposed development, and the strong feelings the people expressed about their homelands and what lay ahead with the mining development.

The Yirrkala people launched an action in the Supreme Court of the Northern Territory against the mining company, claiming that they held a communal native title, recognised by Australian common law, to their traditional lands. Professor Stanner gave expert evidence for the plaintiffs.

In a 1971 decision now known as the *Gove Land Rights Case*, Justice Blackburn of the Northern Territory Supreme Court found that there was a traditional system pertaining to the claimed lands which he described as 'a government of laws and not of men'. Nevertheless his judgement denied that native title was part of Australian common law, and he confirmed the assumed doctrine of *terra nullius*: an empty land without owners.

However, the negative finding in the *Gove Case* combined

with increasing political agitation by Aboriginal people in the early 1970s gave rise to a political imperative to address land rights. If Aboriginal people possessed no inherent rights to land at law, then a moral onus fell upon Parliament to create rights to land. The Woodward Commission, established by the Whitlam Labor Government, eventually led to the enactment of the *Northern Territory Land Rights Act* 1976. This followed moves in South Australia to address land rights.

Similar if increasingly inadequate legislative measures on land title were taken in New South Wales, Victoria and eventually Queensland. As each State eventually dealt with the imperative to address the question of land rights within their jurisdiction, it is true to say that each subsequent measure was less inspired than the last.

What has resulted is a patchwork of legislative regimes which have made provision for some areas of the country and no provision in respect of others. Moves in the mid 1980s at the federal level to introduce a national land rights model failed to fulfil the need for a national provision. The well-spring of goodwill, which erupted after *Gove*, had petered out to a trickle by the time Michael Mansell made his assessment in 1989 that no more would we see land rights legislation in this country. The question, so far as the material Australians of the 1980s were concerned, had been more or less addressed and, if not addressed, then at least attempted. In confirmation of Mansell's assessment, in 1991 the Queensland Labor Party adjusted its land rights policy platform downwards to match its recently introduced legislation. The outcome determined the policy.

It therefore appeared that there would be no more political or social impetus for any national movement on land rights. At this point, Mansell quite correctly asked whether our better prospects lay outside of the nation rather than within it.

The constitutional mandate over Aboriginal Affairs which the 1967 Referendum gave the Commonwealth has been infrequently exercised. Aboriginal Affairs and matters concerning our entitlements have too often been left to the States to repeat the long history of neglect and denial which had given rise to the need for constitutional change in the first place. One of the few assumptions of constitutional responsibility for peoples of the Aboriginal and Torres Strait Islander races was the Whitlam Labor Government's enactment of legislation outlawing Queensland's discriminatory laws. And, of course, the most significant exercise of the race power came in the last days of that Government with the enactment of the *Racial Discrimination Act* in October 1975.

The Act has proved to be pivotal in respect of the protection of native title as established in the *Mabo* cases. The High Court's finding in the 1992 decision, that whilst under Australian common law the British Crown acquired sovereignty over the country, it did not thereby extinguish the beneficial title of the indigenous inhabitants which they held under their own laws and customs, has revolutionised the nation's understanding of its land laws and indeed its history.

There are historical truths which are difficult for some to accept given that history is so important to contemporary political ideology. There are prescriptions which taste like too many bitter pills to many Australians who have alternately lamented, grieved and felt betrayed by the Court's decision.

There may now be some remnant rights which must be accounted for and will no longer suffer denial. This is being met by the complaint of politicians and interest groups that many in the desert areas of Western Australia and elsewhere in remote Australia, where there may be such remnant rights, have not been as comprehensively dispossessed and, better still, obliterated like so many have been in settled Australia. If only their ancestors had achieved in the Pilbara what they achieved in Van Dieman's Land!

There are black Australians too who will also feel betrayed by the Court's decision on native title, who will feel short-changed by history and white law.

But for many Australians, both black and white, *Mabo* represents an opportunity for the achievement of a greater national resolution of the question of Aboriginal land rights, and an improvement in relations between the new and old of this land, a first step in a new direction which might yield the changes necessary for indigenous people to be genuinely re-possessed of their inheritance.

Given the hope and doubt which Aboriginal people feel about the court's decision and the responses of various Governments and the non-Aboriginal public to native title, how can we proceed with feet laden by such trepidation?

Mabo is an attempt by the colonialist legal system to accommodate Aboriginal land rights. It is by no means the most perfect accommodation between rights under Aboriginal law and the white legal system. But, from all assessments, it is close to the best accommodation achievable within the Australian legal system. It stands creditably against similar accommodations in Canada, the United States and New Zealand.

The significance of the decision is that it recognises Aboriginal law and custom as a source of law for the first time in 204 years of colonial settlement. For the great part, however, Aboriginal law remains unrecognised. Nevertheless, the *breadth* of the context of this recognition sets the stage for an interaction which has never before been possible.

Colonial law has been a reality in Australia since 1788. Aboriginal law has always been a reality and we are unanimous in our resolve that it continue to be so. Colonial law is part of our indigenous reality here in Australia; it determines and controls our ability to exercise our law, enjoy our rights, maintain our identities.

With *Mabo*, the colonial system is saying: Yes, we do recognise Aboriginal law in certain circumstances relating to land but our law also says that there has been extinguishment which is legal in many circumstances. As to the balance of Aboriginal law, well, the colonial law is saying: It has no reality, in so far as we are concerned and in so far as we are prepared to act.

No matter the illigitimacy of the imposition of colonial law; no matter how revisionist and how artificial and pragmatic the High Court's recognition of indigenous law in the Murray Island case might be said to be—it is nevertheless the prevailing reality.

They are saying to us: this is the position, this is the reality, what can you do about it?

If this is the situation—that Aboriginal law has restricted recognition and there is little prospect for an extension of recognition through agitation of the common law—what strategies do we pursue to make Aboriginal law have a reality, have consequence for our colonial condition?

For the most part, the Aboriginal political system occupies a sphere which is quite distinct from the white political system. Indigenous political activity and philosophy are largely spinning in an orbit that does not have much relevance to, or impact upon, the dominant sphere in which many of the critical developments are taking place. We need a new political ideology for indigenous political strategy.

Uncle Tom and *Malcolm X* represent the two extreme characterisations of racial-ethnic politics in the United States, where the pan-Afro-American struggle has provided an image of the way black politics ought to be understood. At one end of the spectrum is the sell-out, at the other the radical activist. These characterisations are largely white constructs. The colonists have defined the way in which our struggle is to be understood—they, the media, the wider colonial society, define our struggles as moderate or radical, conservative or activist, to suit themselves, and we have internalised these characterisations and made them our own.

Early black leaders in Australia seized upon the politics of liberating victims which defined the black struggle against segregation in America. The emergence of radical activism changed the way in which Australians were forced to take account of the victims, but it did not always change the stance and the position from which the victims spoke—as the powerless and oppressed minority.

The language of victim politics positioned the rest of Australia as guilty perpetrators. It is an uncomfortable position and not one which will sustain a political cause. The Australian body politic will salve its conscience so far and then react in an indignant backlash, the 'we can't be blamed for what happened' response.

To that constituency, a reminder that such conscience-salving is to be particularly observed in the ready agreement of those most vehemently opposed forces who nevertheless concede the need to address the shameful health, sanitation, educational, employment and housing conditions of black Australians.

Rather than land rights this view urges conscience-salving through the pursuit of what Stanner called the 'hobby horses'. But as in 1968, with many of the statistics deteriorating rather than improving, Stanner's questioning of this approach is relevant to 1993: He said: 'They are all in part right and therefore dangerous. If all these particular measures, with perhaps fifty or a hundred other, were carried out everywhere, simultaneously, and on a sufficient scale, possibly there would be a general advance ... But who shall mobilise and command this regiment of one-eyed hobby horses? And keep them in column?'

For the indigenous quarter, the fact of our changing political circumstances calls for us to re-evaluate our political strategies. People aren't moderates or conservatives on the one hand, and radicals and extremists on the other. Rather, it is actions and strategies which should be seen as moderate or radical. There is a world of difference between black radical cheek and black radical chic. The test of credibility of a strategy is not whether the approach is radical or conservative, but whether it is smart or dumb, and whether it enhances or jeopardises the rights and interests of one's people.

The politics of victims asserts that unless the dominating State accepts us on our own terms, any complicity, any dealing constitutes an unacceptable relinquishment of our power. For a long time, the only political currency which Aboriginal people could use was their refusal to be involved. Now that the non-Aboriginal legal system has offered something in the way of rights, however narrow, to refuse to engage in the game and to fail to appreciate the rules and its limitations—even if our purpose be to disrupt the game—no longer seems smart. The challenge is to negotiate the expansion of those rights without losing ground and without surrendering the chances of future advances in a struggle which has incrementally advanced and whose destination is still long in arriving.